The case against Christ

JOHN YOUNG

FALCON BOOKS · LONDON

First published September 1971
Reprinted 1972
Copyright © John Young 1971

SBN 85491 527 3

Illustrations : Alan Denyer

FALCON BOOKS
are published by CPAS Publications, a department of
the Church Pastoral Aid Society, Falcon Court,
32 Fleet Street, London EC4Y 1DB

Overseas agents
EMU Book Agencies Ltd,
1 Lee Street, Sydney, NSW, Australia

Sunday School Centre Wholesale,
PO Box 3020, Cape Town, South Africa

CSSM and Crusader Bookroom Society Ltd,
177 Manchester Street, Christchurch, New Zealand

Made and printed in Great Britain by
Hunt Barnard Printing Ltd, Aylesbury, Bucks

THE CASE AGAINST CHRIST

Contents

Preface

This book is written in the conviction that the Christian Faith is true. But it is also written in the knowledge that many important objections are frequently raised against it. It is an attempt to act as counsel for the defence in 'The Case Against Christ'.

CHAPTER ONE

Clearing the Decks

Objections to Christianity are nothing new, of course. One of the earliest problems for Christians was the accusation that they were cannibals, because they spoke of 'feeding on Christ' in the Holy Communion. Most twentieth century objectors are rather better informed than this!

Most of the objections we shall examine will require at least one complete chapter, but we shall start by looking at a few problems which can be considered rather more briefly.

It doesn't matter what you believe

'It doesn't matter what you believe as long as you live a good life. It is what you *do* that matters, not what you believe.'

This sort of statement is quite common when people are arguing about religion. The trouble is that it oversimplifies things, for beliefs and actions are tied up together.

If you believe that gods are pleased by human sacrifice (and many people have held this belief) then it is bad luck on your children. If your doctor believes that leeches are the answer to your high temperature, or that a hole bored in the head will cure headaches, it is bad luck on you.

Belief governs action.

Why was it that the Nazis caused such havoc in Europe? It was because they believed that the German people were a super-race, with a destiny to rule the world.

Why did the American government cause such suffering by dropping an atomic bomb on Hiroshima on 6th August, 1945. It was because they believed that this would shorten the war.

This connection between faith and action applies to everything. It is what a man *believes* that makes him an atheist, or a Buddhist, or a Christian, or a communist.

A quotation from 'the little red book' (*Quotations from Mao Tse-tung*) illustrates this clearly. 'We must have faith in the masses and we must have faith in the Party. These are two cardinal principles. If we doubt these principles, we shall accomplish nothing,' says Chairman Mao.

Mr George Watt, a British engineer convicted of spying by a Chinese court, was released on 2nd August, 1970. He pointed out that several other Europeans are being held in an 'ideological reform centre', and said that the communists had tried to brainwash him. They did this in an effort to alter his *beliefs*.

The most brilliant scientist cannot get a government post until he has been security checked. They want to know what he believes. Until they know this, he is regarded as a risk.

Our beliefs are vitally important.

It is boasting to call yourself a Christian

The word 'Christian' is often used as a compliment. I remember hearing someone describe his friend as a communist and an atheist. He added, 'but he is as good a Christian as you or me.' He wanted to say that he thought his friend was a good man, so he used the word 'Christian'.

If this is using the word correctly, then clearly it would be intolerable for anyone to say 'I am a Christian' or 'I became a Christian last year'. It would be the worst kind of boasting. But the follower of Christ does not mean 'I am a specially good person' when he claims to be a Christian.

It is easy to see how the word came to be used in this way. Followers of Christ are expected to lead good lives. But to use the word of all men whom we admire, whether or not they acknowledge Christ, simply causes confusion. After all, His name makes up two thirds of the word.

Many *non*-Christians would agree with this. Lord Ritchie-Calder has done a great deal of good work in such fields as International relations, and the fight against pollution. In 1969 he was given the Victor Gollancz Award for service to humanity. He is a better man than many churchgoers, but he does not wish to be called a Christian, for he does not believe in God.

The word 'Christian' began its life in the New Testament, and it is used there, not as a compliment, but as a *description*. It describes a person who believes that Jesus Christ is the Son of God, and who - sometimes unsuccessfully - tries to follow and worship Him.

This is the way in which the word is used throughout this book. When I call a man a non-Christian, I am not intending to insult him, nor am I suggesting that he is inferior to the man who is a Christian. The phrase is used simply to record the fact that he does not acknowledge Jesus Christ as his Lord and Saviour.

9

Christianity isn't relevant

A fifteen year old boy wrote the following in an essay on 'War':

> 'This is basically due to man's greed and selfishness, and we will never prevent wars until man changes his ways, which I think is impossible ... we will only live peacefully when or until man himself gets rid of his selfish instincts.'

He obviously agrees with the old saying that 'You can't change human nature'. Anything which *could*, would obviously be extremely relevant to life in the twentieth century.

Christians maintain that 'changing human nature' is what Christianity is all about. They claim that Christ is alive today, and that although unseen, He is present and active in our world by His Spirit. If we will allow, He will inject moral and spiritual power into our lives. He will – quite literally – change our human nature, replacing selfishness with love, bitterness with forgiveness, and indifference with active concern.

This is not just 'theory'. Very often the change involved is slow and not very dramatic. But not always. I think of a alcoholic who is now 'dry'; of a depressed person who has scars on his arms from a suicide attempt, whose life is now full of joy and purpose; of a young man who in his teens went to Borstal, detention centre and prison, and who is now training to become a minister in the Church of England.

Why the change? Each of them speaks of the power of Christ in his life.

Is Christianity relevant?

It all happened so long ago
Some people feel that Christianity is too tied up with the past.

Take the Bible. It was written centuries before Shakespeare, and he is difficult enough to understand! How can a book which is about men whose means of transport were limited to horses and camels (or feet!) over land, and wind in sails or oars across the sea, have anything relevant to say to men who can get to the moon?

The trouble with this attitude is that it concentrates on surface differences. If we concentrate on clothes, or customs, or travel, we shall see ourselves as totally different from the men and women we read about in the Bible, and conclude that the Bible cannot say anything useful today.

But in fact the *similarities* between the Bible characters and ourselves are enormous. The problems they faced were basically *our* problems – the cost of living, war and peace, getting on with other people, and so on. We find in the Bible people who fell in love, people who hated, people who were anxious and afraid, people who worked, people who laughed and cried, people who fell ill, people who grew old, people who died.

The Bible is about men and women like that, and activities like that. It deals with the 'constants' in human life, and deals with them in a profound way.

It was a book for the first century. It is a book for the twentieth century. It is a book for all ages.

The same thing applies to Christ. He is a man for all ages. He is, of course, an historical character – but this does not mean that He cannot affect our lives now. Many things which happened in history affect our lives today tremendously – the formation of coal and the discovery of radio waves for example. Events in the past *do* affect the present.

Last century Sir James Young Simpson devoted himself to fighting the evil of disease. He gave the world anaesthetics, which are, of course, still highly important. (Just imagine living in a world without modern, painless surgery.)

Twenty centuries ago Jesus Christ devoted Himself to

fighting the evils of sin and death. The work of both these men was done in the past, but the work of both of them has consequences in the present.

The climax of Christ's fight against evil was on the cross, where He took on Himself the awful consequences of the world's sin. But that was not the end, for God raised Him from the dead.

It is His *Resurrection* which makes Christ vitally relevant in any age. You are alive today because of a past event – your birth. Christ is alive today because of a past event – His Resurrection from the dead.

If we think of Christ *only* as a figure in history we are wrong, for He lives in the present too. It is not just that He lived *then*. He lives *now* as well.

Christianity is still relevant today, because Christ is still alive.

Christians are odd

Some people are put off Christianity because they feel that Christians are rather odd people.

Pop singer Sandie Shaw is reported to have said, 'I don't go to church and all that crap. Well I mean, you meet such cranky people who do. The Church seems to attract them. I'm sure Christianity was alright in the beginning, but not now.'

It is true of course that the Church does attract some odd characters. I remember taking a smart young lady to a 'fashionable' church in the West End of London, hoping to interest her in Christianity.

Unfortunately an elderly gentleman decided to attend the same church. He spent the whole time putting his boots on and off. And you didn't need to *see* what he was doing to know this!

The fact that our churches attract some odd people shouldn't surprise us. We should expect a community which really cares for people, to attract people who *need* to be cared for.

But this isn't the complete picture by any means, and I suspect that if those who think Christians are odd really got to know a group of Christians, they would probably be surprised to discover how normal and healthy they are.

Nevertheless, the fact remains that Christians *are* different from other people in certain respects. Judged by usual standards, some of their interests *are* decidedly strange - prayer, worship and self-sacrifice, for example.

I was recently talking to a fifteen stone man who had been a prisoner of war in the Far East. He, and most of his friends in the prison camp, were about seven stone then. They were so used to living with very thin, undernourished people, that when the first soldiers from the British Army of liberation arrived, they thought that they were terribly fat and bloated. In fact of course, the soldiers were healthy people. It was *they* who were fully alive, and the prisoners who were only just existing.

It is possible that this is the case when non-Christians look at Christians today. They notice that the Christians are different, and assume that it is they (the Christians) who are odd. But this estimate could be wrong. Perhaps the Christians are in fact on the way to becoming the really healthy human beings which God intends us all to be.

Religion is dull

Agreed! Mere religion is dull. But Christianity, *the real thing* that is, is not. It involves a vital dynamic relationship with a living person, and that is never dull.

If someone at a wedding drinks lemonade, believing it to be champagne, he may think that champagne is dull. But he will be wrong, for he is passing judgment on the wrong thing.

Most people have had some experience of 'religion'. And they have found it boring. The repetition, the old-fashioned language, the dressing up, the lack of enthusiasm in the singing, the suspected insincerity - things like this have put them off. On the other hand, fewer people have experienced living, vital, Christianity. But because of their experience of religion, very many dismiss Christianity, for they think these are the same thing.

It is rather like a vaccination. You can be prevented from catching the real thing, by a smaller dose of something similar.

Jesus said, 'I have come that men may have life, and may have it in all its fullness' (John 10. 10).

He speaks of a new quality of life, which all Christian people - but not all 'religious' people - have.

Dynamite is pretty dull stuff until you put a light to the charge. Religion is dull when it is dead. It is Christ who brings it to life. *He* can transform mere religion into vital adventurous faith. When He does so, the outward expressions of that faith : church going, prayer, bible reading etc. - come to life as well.

There is all the difference in the world between formal religion and real Christianity.

We have looked at some of the objections which are raised against Christianity, and will be considering several more. The danger with this is that it may give the impression of a defensive 'back to the wall' attitude.

In fact of course, Christians are not alone in finding it necessary to discuss problems raised by their beliefs. For example, a group of Agnostics recently published a book entitled 'Objections to Humanism', in which they spoke of the difficulties which *they* face as a result of their beliefs.

Every view of life raises problems and it is important that these problems should be faced and discussed.

CHAPTER TWO

Christians are no better than anyone else

Two women were talking at the bus-stop. 'Such goings on. And her a regular church-goer too.' They clearly thought that Christians should be better than other people, but that in practice, some at least, are not.

Most of the objections which are raised when people are arguing about religion are concerned with straight thinking. Phrases like 'Prove it'; 'Where's your evidence?' 'Is it true?' are used.

But there is at least one objection which is essentially *practical*. Christians, it is said, don't practise what they preach. They are no better than anyone else.

This objection is true in one very important sense. Christians are *not* good people. They know they are not, and it is for this very reason that they find Jesus Christ so important.

Christ is not just a great teacher, or a fine example. In the Bible He is often called a Saviour. The word means 'Saver' or 'Rescuer'. He saves people from their selfishness, their indifference to the needs of others, their pride, jealousy, snobbishness, lust and so on – those things which spoil our lives, and which sometimes makes us ashamed.

Jesus spoke of himself as a Doctor. 'It is not the healthy that need a doctor, but the sick,' he said. 'I did not come to invite virtuous people, but sinners' (Mark 2. 17). Christians are sinners who have responded to this invitation.

When Christians go to church, they are not trying to impress other people with their uprightness and goodness. This would be like going to a hospital to show how healthy you are! One of the first prayers in a Church of England Service contains the phrase 'there is no health in us'. Each church is like an outpatients' department in a hospital for the spiritually and morally sick.

The marvel is, not that the church fails so often but that it has done any good at all, considering it is made up of self-confessed moral failures.

A Christian is not a basically good, respectable, religious person. He is a thoroughly dissatisfied person. He is dissatisfied with *himself*. He knows that he is selfish; or that he cannot control his temper; or that he is jealous; or greedy; or lazy; or...It is because he knows his own shortcomings, and his own great need, that he has gone to the one Person who can help him – Jesus Christ, the Great Physician.

But sometimes a cure takes a long time. Especially when someone has a really bad dose of an illness. Sometimes the phrase 'Christians are no better than other people' is not true because it does not go far enough. Some Christians are a lot *worse* by ordinary standards.

There are, for example, criminals, drug addicts, and

alcoholics who are real Christians. Their lives are not always changed in a flash. Sometimes it is a long uphill struggle. But because the cure depends on the strength of Christ and not the individual Christian, a successful outcome is certain in the long run. The disease of sin, no matter how severe, will always be healed eventually, if the person gives himself totally into Christ's hands.

The trouble is that we all have something wrong with us, and an apparently mild attack, if left untreated, will get steadily worse.

So far we have assumed that those being criticized are real Christians. This might not always be the case. Many people, especially during those periods when the Church was very influential, became involved in the life of the Church for false reasons. Perhaps for power, or prestige, or money or reputation.

There have been traitors in the camp. Men very far from the Spirit of Christ, and with total disregard for the teaching of Christ, have sometimes joined the Church of Christ. This was inevitable during those centuries when everyone in a European country was automatically regarded as a Christian.

There are many bad and evil things in the history of the Church - the tortures of the Inquisition; the burning of innocent men simply because they were Protestants; the beheading of innocent men simply because they were Catholics; the unwillingness of many in the Church to fight against social injustice during the last century.

Some of these terrible things came about because true Christian men are still sinful men, and always share a good deal of the prejudice and ignorance of the age in which they live. But some of them came about because non-Christian men held positions of importance in the Church. These were men who were concerned not with following Christ, but only with their own comfort, power and security. For such men, modern Christians have no need to apologize.

The credit side

If we think only of the Inquisition, the quarrels between Roman Catholics and Protestants in Northern Ireland, the dullness of many church services, the constant begging for money, or the refusal of many church-goers to 'get involved', we shall, alas, be thinking about facts. But not *all* the facts.

If Christ really does help His followers to overcome their selfishness, and if He really does pour His love into their lives, we should expect to see some practical evidence of this in the lives of at least some Christians.

We are not disappointed. There *is* a credit side. The failures are great, but the successes are tremendous too. There are enough men and women who have done great things *because* of their Christian faith, to show that the statement, 'Christians are no better than anyone else' is not always true. Here are a few examples:

Dr Barnardo (1845–1905)

When he was converted to Christ as a young man, Thomas John Barnardo resolved to go to China as a medical missionary. It was while he was studying medicine in order to do this that he discovered the 'ragged children' of London.

He discovered that there were dozens of children – young children – who had no homes, no parents, no work, no hope.

One night he discovered 11 youngsters sleeping on a roof, in the shelter of a high wall. On another occasion he found 73 children sleeping under a tarpaulin in Billingsgate Fish Market.

He could have shrugged his shoulders, as very many did, and dismissed the problem as none of his business, or as too big to solve. But he was trying to follow Christ, who said, 'Let the children come to me,' and, 'give to the poor'.

Barnardo decided to help these children. He decided that

he could best serve God in London, not in China.

'No destitute child ever refused admission.' This became Barnardo's motto, and it was heroic considering that London was alive with poverty-stricken children.

Even the motto was the result of tragedy. A boy called 'Carrots' was given money and told to return later. He did not return, because he died of exposure – hence the motto.

Until his death in 1905 some 60,000 youngsters passed through Barnardo's care. Today the total is over 165,000. With over 8,000 children at any one time, Barnardo's is the largest family in the world.

Lord Shaftesbury (1801–1885)

A devout Christian and an influential MP, he devoted his life to getting a better deal for ordinary men and women. The Bible teaches constantly about the need for social justice, and Lord Shaftesbury put these passages into practice.

At a time when young children worked from seven in the morning until late at night, and when most people from the middle and upper classes accepted this as necessary, Shaftesbury opposed it totally.

He was a wealthy man, who could have joined others of his class in leading a life of idle luxury. But Christ was his Master, and he could not rest with social injustice all around him.

Factory workers, miners, chimney climbing boys, 'ragged' children (Shaftesbury knew and helped Barnardo), flower girls, prostitutes, criminals, the mentally sick – these all benefited from his deep concern for their suffering, and from the laws which he pushed through, often in the teeth of great opposition.

London's Shaftesbury Avenue is named after him, and one of the world's most famous statues – Eros in Picadilly Circus – is dedicated to him.

The Burning of Widows

William Carey sailed to India in 1793 as a Baptist Missionary, He remained there until his death in 1834.

Despite his lack of formal education (he was a shoemaker by trade), Carey was a brilliant linguist who spent a great deal of time on translation work. Sometimes he translated the whole Bible, sometimes just selected passages. In all, he produced translations into 25 languages and dialects.

His concern was not just to translate the Bible into words, but to translate its teaching into practical terms. One custom which he fought was Suttee, which required widows to die in the flames which cremated the bodies of their husbands. Carey worked and prayed to get the custom stopped, and in 1829 he succeeded.

Slavery

For 350 years slaves were shipped across the Atlantic from Africa to the Americas. Slaves were regarded as cargo. The slave traders were in it for money, and the more slaves they carried, the bigger the returns.

The lower deck of one French ship captured in 1822 contained 250 slaves. They were packed into an area 20 feet by 50 feet. This means that each slave had an allocation of four square feet – about half the area of the not very large table at which I am now writing. The journey took about five weeks.

Such conditions were not uncommon.

Little wonder that more than 10 out of every 100 slaves died on the journey. (i.e. about 40,000 deaths each year). Little wonder that some went mad on the journey. Little wonder there were epidemics. Little wonder that the 'British sailors came to dread the moment when the hatches were lifted and they peered into the slave decks, with their appalling stench, and heard the cries of the sick and wounded in the crammed quarters' (Quoted from the *Observer* colour supplement, 17 October 1965).

The man who did more than anyone else in England to outlaw slavery was William Wilberforce, another MP whose Christian conscience would not allow him to rest until such evil was stopped. He was encouraged by John Wesley, the founder of the Methodist Church.

But slavery meant wealth for many in England, and Wilberforce had a long, bitter fight against important opponents like Lord Nelson. It was a struggle to which he believed he was called by Christ. And so it was a struggle which he would not give up. And it was a struggle which he won.

It is very sad that a shadow has been cast over Wilberforce's reputation by those who maintain that he was interested in the suffering of slaves far away, but not of Englishmen near at hand. This is simply not true. The historian Bishop Stephen Neill has written, 'Legend dies hard; but this cannot stand against the most cursory study of the evidence.'

We have looked at four examples from the last century, because it was a century when so much needed to be done. The power of Christ in the lives of men has continued into the twentieth century, however, as the following examples show.

Christians Against Hitler

When Hitler came to power in Germany, he tried to use the Church to gain support. To their shame, some churchmen agreed, not seeing the monstrous shape of things to come.

But some refused to cooperate. They formed the 'Confessing Church' in Germany, and throughout the entire period of Hitler's power, they opposed him.

E. H. Robertson, an expert on the Church in Germany during the war period, has written:

'The resistance of the Confessing Church to the policy of Hitler continued into and through the war years. It alone survived the bitter attack on all opposition and non-conformity, and raised its voice constantly in 2,000 pulpits and in every possible way.'

Leprosy

Christians continue to go overseas in large numbers, to work in underdeveloped countries. Teaching, agriculture, building, medical work – these are some of the fields to which they contribute with distinction.

Special mention should be given to the immense contribution made by Christian missionaries in the field of leprosy. One Society – the Leprosy Mission – specializes entirely in this work, but other Missionary Societies are also involved.

A famous name in this area is Father Damien, a Roman Catholic priest, who worked among leprosy sufferers in the days before a cure was known. They were treated as outcasts, and Father Damien's work on the Hawaiian Island of Molokai involved building houses, and providing a water supply, in addition to elementary medical care. He contracted leprosy himself in 1885, and died in 1889, at the age of 49.

Since then enormous progress has been made. The Vellore Christian Medical College and Hospital in India is a leading leprosy unit, and was one of the centres which did research into the development of sulphone drugs. These drugs, especially dapsone or DDS, have become central in the treatment of leprosy.

Dr Paul Brand has worked at Vellore for many years and is now the Director of Surgery and Rehabilitation of the Leprosy Mission. He has pioneered techniques in reconstructive surgery on hands and feet, for leprosy often causes deformity.

Africa is another leprosy area. In July 1970, Dr Stanley Browne was awarded the Royal African Society's Medal for dedicated service to that continent. The Council spoke of his 'unrivalled knowledge of leprosy research, treatment and control'. Among other things, Dr Browne is Medical Consultant to the Leprosy Mission.

The Christian Church, through its missionary societies, has made a massive contribution to this field, but the task is still enormous. It is estimated that of the twelve to fifteen million leprosy sufferers in the world today, only about two and a half million are receiving treatment.

In
DISTRESS
or
DESPAIR
ring
SAMARITANS
Phone :

– – – –

Suicide

In Britain each year there are approximately 6,000 cases of suicide. In addition, at least 30–40,000 attempt suicide. Professor Stengel, a psychiatrist with a specialist knowledge of this subject, has written, 'Neither the triumphs of scientific medicine nor the rise in the standard of living have curbed loss of life through suicide. They have, on the contrary, tended to increase it.'

The Samaritans is an organization which was started by a London rector, the Rev. Chad Varah, in 1953, to help those people who felt so depressed that they considered 'putting an end to it all'. People in this frame of mind were invited to ring Mansion House 9000.

Samaritans has grown into an international movement and it is no longer a specifically Christian organization, although many Christians are still involved. Men and women of all faiths are invited to become helpers, provided they are willing to give their time, and are prepared to listen to the troubles of others.

This is by no means an isolated example of a Christian starting something which has snowballed beyond the limits of the Church.

Shelter

This organization was formed on 1 December, 1966, in order to combat the enormous misery and suffering caused by the large, but often unnoticed problem of homelessness in Britain. It now helps to rehouse an average of about fifty families each week.

It is *not* a specifically Christian organization, but it finds a place here because Christians were prominent among those who formed it. This is clearly seen from the fact that *Shelter* came into being as a result of the united concern of five organizations – the Notting Hill Housing Trust, the Catholic Housing Aid Society, The National Federation of Housing Societies, Christian Action, and the British Churches Housing Trust.

Of the five individuals singled out for special mention by *Shelter* in connection with the launching of the Movement, one is a Roman Catholic (Father Eamonn Casey, now Bishop of Kerry), one is a Quaker (Lewis E. Waddilove) and one is a Congregationalist Minister. The latter, Bruce Kenrick, was the first Chairman of *Shelter*.

Missing Persons

In any list concerned with the social action of Christians, the Salvation Army must find a place. The work of that organization among 'down and outs' is probably its best known activity, but of course it does a great deal more than this, with well over 3,000 full time officers devoted to social work.

For many years, the Salvation Army has regarded the fact that large numbers of people simply 'disappear', as a human problem requiring specialist knowledge. Every year their Missing Persons Bureau helps restore some 5,000 people to lost relatives. Their total successes in this field amount to more than 250,000.

The Quakers
The keen sense of social concern demonstrated by the Quakers in such areas as prison reform is well known. In addition, they have remained resolute in their refusal to fight in a war. But this has not meant a negative opting out. The Friends Ambulance Unit run by the Quakers during the Second World War, served both sides with courage and dignity, and earned widespread respect.

World Hunger
The television screen has made us aware of the fact that more than one half of the world is hungry. Almost every time your heart beats, someone dies of malnutrition.

The only way to solve this problem is for large numbers of countries to agree to combat it, at the very highest government level.

Meanwhile, there is a great deal that can be done by Voluntary Organizations. To say that the Church is making a major contribution to this field would be untrue, for the problem is so vast that no voluntary organization can make a *major* contribution.

Through Christian Aid, the Catholic Fund for Overseas Development (CAFOD), the Evangelical Alliance Relief (TEAR Fund) and the Missionary Societies, the Churches pour millions of pounds into this problem each year.

At least *some* of that money for which the Church is always said to be asking, is given away.

We must stop there with the list incomplete. If there had been no Jesus Christ, and hence no Christian Church, would the world be any poorer?

Ask the workers of the last century; ask the homeless children; ask the slaves; ask the women of India; ask those suffering from leprosy; ask the despairing; ask the homeless; ask the starving:

And then ask *yourself*.

Books of interest

Ten Fingers for God by Dorothy Clarke Wilson (Hodder and Stoughton):
the story of the surgeon Paul Brand, and his work among leprosy sufferers

Christians and Social Work by I. Birnie (Arnold)

CHAPTER THREE

Science has disproved religion

Can a scientist be a Christian?

'But surely, Sir, science has disproved God.' This sentence was addressed by a sixth-former to Professor Coulson, the Oxford mathematician. The fact that the Professor is not only a leading scientist but also a Christian (he is a past Vice-President of the Methodist Conference) was something which that schoolboy could not sort out. In suggesting that Science and Religion are opposed he was speaking for a good many people.

In fact, the particular combination found in Dr Coulson – Scientist *and* Christian – has not been uncommon throughout the history of science.

Many of the founders of modern science were men with

27

a firm belief in God. Galileo Galilei (1564–1642) and Sir Isaac Newton (1642–1727) are good examples.

Newton has been called 'the greatest British scientist of all time'. Books about him continue to be written. In addition to giving us his famous 'laws of motion' he contributed brilliantly to the fields of optics, astronomy and that branch of mathematics called differential calculus, among other things. Yet Newton wrote theological as well as scientific books, and regarded his theological works as more important.

Galileo, another brilliant early scientist, was persecuted by the Catholic Church for his scientific views, but this was not a question of an atheist fighting the Christians. Galileo was a devout Catholic who believed in God just as much as the Church leaders. It was a clash between two views on authority and the correct approach to truth (although of course, this doesn't excuse the Church leaders for their attitude in the affair).

From a later period we may single out Michael Faraday (1791–1867) who discovered electromagnetism, Sir James Young Simpson (1811–1870) who discovered the anaesthetic properties of chloroform, and hence paved the way for painless surgery, and Lord Joseph Lister (1822–1912) who pioneered antiseptic surgery, and saved thousands of lives and a great deal of suffering. Each of these men was deeply religious, in addition to being a brilliant scientist. Simpson was asked to name his greatest discovery. He is reported to have replied, 'It was not chloroform. My greatest discovery has been to know that I am a sinner and that I could be saved by the grace of God.'

Gregor Mendel (1822–84) the Austrian monk whose researches into the laws of heredity form the basis of the modern science of genetics, and Louis Pasteur (1822–95) the French chemist who gave his name to pasteurized milk are two further examples.

The 'Scientist and Christian' combination continues

today. Several top professional scientists in addition to Professor Coulson are convinced Christians who have written about the relationship between Science and Christianity. Donald M. MacKay, Professor of Communication at Keele University (he is an expert on the workings of the human brain and the theory of computers); Frank H. T. Rhodes, Professor of Geology at Michigan University; Malcolm Jeeves, Professor of Psychology at St Andrew's University; Douglas Spanner, Reader in Biology at London University, and Robert L. F. Boyd, Professor of Physics at University College London, and until 1969 Professor of Astronomy at the Royal Institution, are distinguished examples. And it is worth recording that The Research Scientists Christian Fellowship has some 700 members.

What is the significance of all this? Let us be clear what the significance is *not*. This list of names does *not* prove that Christianity is true. If every scientist in the world was a practising Christian it would not prove this. The evidence for Christianity is to be found in the areas of history and personal experience, not in science - although the evidence is none the less important or impressive for this.

Not that all scientists *are* Christians of course; far from it. Convinced Christians are in a minority in almost any job (except among clergymen we hope!) and we would not expect to find that a majority of scientists are Christians, any more than we would expect a majority of bus drivers or school teachers to be Christians. And of course, it is well known that some scientists have recorded their *dis*-belief in Christianity. Professor Fred Hoyle of Cambridge University is a notable example.

What the information *does* show is that Christianity and Science are not opposed. The sixth-former is wrong. If two sides really are competing against each other, no player can be on both sides at once.

And if we will allow that most scientists are intelligent men, the fact that a fair number of scientists are Christians also suggests that Christianity is not just an old wives' tale, suitable only for those who cannot think for themselves. This was backed up by a recent survey in which approximately 45% of the members of British Mensa declared a Church affiliation. (Mensa is a society open only to those who have an IQ which is higher than 98% of the general population.)

Charles Darwin and all that

If it is true that Christianity and Science are not opposed, why do so many people think that they are? The probable reason is that there *was* a clash between them. While most theologians, and most scientists who are interested in the question, maintain that the conflict is a thing of the past, popular opinion lags several years behind expert opinion in this, as in every field of human life. The time of real conflict was about a hundred years ago. It was in 1859 that Charles Darwin published his book *The Origin of Species by Means of Natural Selection* in which he put forward the view that life on earth has evolved into higher and higher forms over a long period. But the early chapters of *Genesis* give a different explanation. We read there that God created the world in six days.

If Darwin is right, the Bible must be wrong, it was reasoned.

Some non-Christians took this view. So did some Christians, and although other Christians like F. J. A. Hort, the Cambridge theologian, welcomed Darwin's researches in the name of truth, there was an almighty rumpus.

It is most interesting to notice where Charles Darwin himself stood in all this.

Because of the controversy caused by his book, he is often thought to be one of the great enemies of the Christian Faith. In fact he was very sympathetic to Christianity. In *Origin of Species* and in his later book *The Descent of Man* he made it clear that he had no intention of attacking

Christianity. He spoke about 'The Creator' and used a quotation which spoke of the need to study 'God's word' and 'God's works'.

Lord Tennyson, the poet, asked Darwin whether his theory of evolution attacked Christianity, and Darwin replied 'No, certainly not.'

This statement is reinforced by Darwin's attitude to missionary work. He had travelled widely on *HMS Beagle*, gathering material for scientific research. During the five year voyage the ship had visited Tierra del Fuego, at the southern tip of South America.

Darwin knew, therefore, that the inhabitants of that island were very primitive and savage. When he heard that Christian missionaries were going there, he thought that they were bound to fail. He was wrong, and was humble enough to admit it.

In 1870 he wrote to the South American Missionary Society – an Anglican Society which continues to do great work today.

'The success of the Tierra del Fuego Mission is most wonderful, and charms me, as I always prophesied utter failure. It is a grand success. I shall feel proud if your committee think fit to elect me an honorary member of your society.'

And so we find Charles Darwin, eleven years after the publication of his most controversial book, in the unexpected role of a supporter of Christian missionary work – compelled to that position by the sheer weight of the evidence of the power of Christianity in action.

What then of Genesis?

'In the beginning God created the heavens and the earth...'
It was these opening verses of the Bible which were read

to the world by the Apollo 8 team as they circled the moon on Christmas Day 1968.

If it is true that the argument between science and Christianity has lost its heat, how has it been resolved? In particular, how are we to view those accounts of Creation in *Genesis* which were at the centre of the controversy?

This is one of those areas where we find a variety of opinions among Christians.

1. Some maintain that these chapters in *Genesis* are to be taken literally. As far as they are concerned, the battle is still on. If the theory of evolution appears to clash with the Bible, so much the worse for the theory of evolution. They point out (quite rightly) that it is still the *theory* not the *fact* of evolution, that Darwin's views have been considerably modified by later scientists, and that some biologists have strong reservations about accepting the theory at all.

The surgeon Sir Cecil Wakely (a past President of the Royal College of Surgeons) is a leading representative of this viewpoint. He maintains that 'there is no evidence, scientific or otherwise, to support the theory of evolution.' He speaks about 'exposing the unproved theory of evolution, and establishing the proved Biblical fact of the Creation of mankind.' Clearly, views held by men of such eminence, on subjects which they have studied closely, are to be respected.

2. Many Christians strongly disagree with this approach. They point out that the majority of biologists think that there are good grounds for accepting the theory of evolution, and they maintain that it is quite possible to accept this theory *and* the Bible. The Bible tells us *that* God created the world and all living creatures. Modern scientific theories like evolution attempt to tell us *how* He did it. They may go on to point out that the order of Creation in *Genesis* is very similar to that suggested by scientists investigating the origins of life on earth (e.g. water creatures before animals). They may suggest that the six 'days' of creation in *Genesis* represent very long periods of time.

32

3. Other Christians agree broadly with this view, but believe that even the points about order and time are not really important. They maintain that it is essential to view *Genesis* as *pre*-scientific or *non*-scientific literature. It was written centuries before the rise of modern science, and it is therefore unimportant whether or not it squares with the findings of scientists, for the writer was not concerned with modern scientific questions.

Genesis and modern science do not *agree* or *disagree* with each other, because they use different types of language, and are concerned with different problems. Dr Alan Richardson represents this viewpoint when he says that Genesis 'is dealing with matters beyond the scope of science.'

Central to these last two views is the idea that *literal* truth is not the only real truth. We are of course, quite used to accepting statements as true, even though we would not dream of taking them literally.

| I lost my head | She's an old battle-axe |
| I smell a rat | He's got a frog in his throat |

When Robert Burns wrote 'O my Luve's like a red, red rose' we understand that he did not mean that every embrace was extremely painful, or that her complexion suggested she was prone to nose-bleeds!

The same principle applies to the parables of Jesus. Did the Prodigal Son or the Good Samaritan exist outside the imagination of Jesus? Did he really know of a widow who kept going to a judge, or a woman who lost a coin? Perhaps; perhaps not. It simply does not matter. We would not accuse Jesus of lying, if he invented these characters to illustrate the truths he wanted to communicate. To do so would be like refusing to take a novel seriously because the characters are fictitious. Parables and novels can teach profound truths without being *literally* true.

The same approach can be applied to the early chapters of *Genesis*. We can believe that the writer of *Genesis* was inspired by God, without maintaining that *Genesis* is intended to give a literal and scientifically exact account of the way in which the world began. We must not judge it as though this was the intention. *But it is true*. It teaches vitally important truths about God, mankind, and the world in which we live.

God created the world. Man is the 'crown' of God's Creation. He was given a measure of real freedom. He rebelled against God. (This is the main significance of the Adam and Eve stories.) This rebellion affected the subsequent history of the world, and can be seen in all human relationships today. All these truths are found in those first few chapters of the Bible. They are expressed there with a superbly poetic artistry which can be understood by men of all ages and cultures.

On the basis of reading *Genesis* and taking it seriously but not literally, what sort of world would we expect to find? We would expect a world in which there is a great deal of beauty and design, plus a great deal of trouble and disharmony. In short, we would expect to find the world *as it actually is*.

This is the genius of the book of *Genesis*. It describes and explains the human situation in a most profound way. The glory and the tragedy are both there. The rest of the Bible shows the solution to the great problems raised there – man's disharmony with God and with his fellow men – being worked out.

Such literature is every bit as important as a scientific treatise on the origins of the universe.

CHAPTER FOUR

Christianity and Science

There are basically three views of the relationship between
Science and Christianity. The 'antagonistic view' suggests
that science has disproved religion, and we examined that in
the previous chapter. In this chapter we consider the other
two views.

God is in there Somewhere

Some Christians, knowing that scientists are explaining
more and more, look anxiously for gaps in scientific knowledge, and maintain that God is at work in these gaps in a

way which is beyond scientific explanation. In this way they hope to defend the existence of God in a scientific age. We cannot do without God, they maintain, for the gaps in scientific knowledge can only be accounted for by His activity. For obvious reasons, this view is sometimes called 'the God of the gaps'.

It is a fatal approach for two reasons:

(1) The gaps in scientific knowledge are still enormous but they are shrinking all the time. What was a large gap ten years ago may be a very small gap, or even no gap at all, now. Hence God appears to be squeezed out.

1970   **1980**   **1990**

Area understood by scientists

A gap in scientific understanding

(2) This view is based on a false understanding of the relationship between God and His creation. The Bible teaches that God is 'behind' or 'upholds' the *whole* of Creation, not just the puzzling parts. He is every bit as responsible for those areas which *can* be explained by scientists, as those which (as yet anyway) *cannot*. In the diagram, the white area is God's handiwork, as well as the shaded areas.

This defensive view, or God of the gaps, is as false as the antagonistic view.

Two ways of looking at the same thing

This is by far the most satisfactory approach to the problem as the large majority of those who write on this subject would agree. They maintain that Christianity and Science view and explain things from two *different*, but *equally valid*, angles.

A few everyday examples will illustrate the principle behind this approach. Some of these examples may at first sight seem to be a long way away from the question under discussion, but we shall end up there eventually.

People

A recent newspaper article suggested that Miss World is in reality a collection of chemicals, of total value about £1. We see from this the importance of taking more than one viewpoint into account. And it shows the danger of phrases like 'nothing but', 'only' and 'merely'.

Miss World, like the rest of us, *is* a collection of chemicals. But she is not *only* or *nothing but* a group of chemicals. Ask the television audience!

It is perfectly valid to view human beings from the point of view of their chemical composition. It is *not* valid to suggest that this is the only viewpoint.

Similarly, it can be useful to think of a man as a machine (which he is) or an advanced animal (which he is), as long as we don't think that by describing him in these terms we have made it impossible to describe him from any other viewpoint – a spiritual viewpoint, for example. To say that man is an animal is one thing. To say that man is *only* an animal is something quite different.

Objects

Almost any object can be viewed from a variety of viewpoints which complement, or add to, one another. A diamond may be regarded by a millionaire as an article giving prestige, by a geologist as a piece of very hard native crystallized carbon, and by an engaged couple as a symbol of their intention to marry. To ask *whose* viewpoint is right is to ask a nonsense question. They are *all* correct.

Events
Events can be explained from different viewpoints as well. They can be described in *scientific* terms and in *personal* terms.

A window is broken. Why?
Answer in scientific terms:
When a missile weighing four ounces travelling at 60 miles per hour strikes a pane of glass $\frac{1}{8}''$ thick, the inevitable result is that the glass will shatter.
Answer in personal terms:
Johnny Green has made a catapult.

Johnny Green is crying. Why?
Answer in scientific terms:
When a missile the weight of a man's hand and travelling at 40 miles per hour, strikes the skin, the nerve ends are aggravated in such a way as to cause extreme discomfort.
Answer in personal terms:
Johnny Green's Dad was so wild when he received the bill for a new window, that he slapped his son's rump vigorously.

To ask which of these explanations is correct is clearly absurd. It is not a question of either/or. We have two completely different explanations and *both are correct*.

One of the explanations may be more *appropriate* to the situation than the other. If you had given Johnny's Dad the scientific explanation to his angry question about the broken window, he would have been even more angry. But both explanations are true, even though only one is sufficiently relevant to be worth stating.

This principle applies to everything. Why is the kettle boiling? When the temperature of water is raised to 100°C (at standard pressure), extremely rapid evaporation takes place. Why is the kettle boiling? It is 4 o'clock, and old Mrs Brown always makes a cup of tea at that time.

And so we could go on. But we must return to the central question. What has this to do with science and religion?

What applies to everyday events – the broken window, the boiling kettle – can be applied to the really big events as well.

Why does the earth support life? It is quite possible to give an answer in scientific terms. Factors like the importance of carbon, and the size of the earth being just right to support an atmosphere will be mentioned. But it is equally possible to give an explanation in 'personal' terms, by maintaining that God deliberately designed the earth so that these factors apply. If this is the case, then scientists are simply discovering the way in which God has designed the world, and so helping us to see His greatness.

Hence Sir James Jeans could speak of God as a mathematician, and Kepler, the brilliant early astronomer, could say that he was 'thinking God's thoughts after Him'. Dr Malcolm Dixon, a biochemist, puts it clearly. 'If we believe that God made the worlds, have we the slightest ground for saying that He did not do it through the operation of natural laws and natural forces?...Surely not.'

It is, of course, open to anyone to disagree with the explanation in terms of the activity of God. Others may wish to explain it as the work of chance not the work of God. But it is not open to anyone to disagree with the explanation in terms of God *because* science can explain why the earth supports life.

The fact that science can give an explanation does not and cannot disprove the explanation in personal terms, any more than the scientific explanation for Johnny Green's stinging bottom, proves that his father did not hit him.

The two explanations are complementary. They can live happily together.

Science does not disprove religion. Nor does it prove it. It simply looks at things in a different way.

Concluding quotations

'Science without religion is blind, religion without science is lame' – Albert Einstein (the scientist who revolutionized modern Physics with his 'Theory of Relativity')

'During the past thirty years people from all the civilized countries of the earth have consulted me...Among all my patients in the second half of life – that is to say over thirty-five – there has not been one whose problem in the last resort was not that of finding a religious outlook on life' – Carl Gustav Jung (One of the great founders of Psychology)

'Religion and natural science are fighting a joint battle in an incessant, never relaxing crusade against scepticism and against dogmatism, against disbelief and against superstition, and the rallying cry in this crusade has always been, and always will be: "On to God" ' – Max Planck (awarded the Nobel Prize for Physics for his work on the Quantum Theory)

Books of interest

Science and Christian Belief by C. A. Coulson (Fontana)

Christianity in a Mechanistic Universe edited by D. M. Mackay (IVP)

Creation and Evolution by D. C. Spanner (Falcon Books)

CHAPTER FIVE

You can't believe the Bible today

A good many people feel fairly sure that the Bible has been 'disproved'. A best seller? Certainly. Interesting? Possibly. But when it comes to the really important question of truth – more fiction than fact.

If they are right, this is extremely damaging to the Christian Faith, for we are largely dependent upon the New Testament for our information about Christ.

Did Jesus really exist?

We are largely dependent on the New Testament for our information about Christ, but not *entirely* dependent. There were other men who lived very near to the time of Jesus who wrote about him.

41

Pliny an official of the Roman Empire, who executed some Christians in about AD 100 was one. Josephus (approx AD 37–100), an official historian, was another.

From these, and from other writings not found in the Bible, we can be quite sure that Jesus lived, that He was executed by crucifixion, and that His followers made a tremendous impact on the world through their firm conviction that God had raised Him from the dead. Professor W. D. Davies, of Columbia University has written: 'The existence of Jesus as a historical figure is not now seriously questioned'. C. J. Cadoux, another New Testament scholar, commenting on the view that Jesus did not really exist wrote: 'The idea is quite fantastic, and has not been championed so far as I know, by any competent historian'.

For a more detailed account of the life of Jesus we must of course depend on the New Testament, so the question as to whether this gives us an accurate record of His life and teaching is still extremely important. Christianity demands that we drastically alter our lives, and we are right to demand in return that it should produce strong credentials.

The procedure for assessing the reliability of the New Testament is the same as for any other important ancient document the original of which has been lost. There are two vital factors, both of which depend on the discovery of old copies of the document.

The first factor involves the *number* of copies which have been found. The second concerns the *age* of these copies – the time lag between the original document and the copies which now exist.

Take, for example, an ancient battle. Details of the battle were recorded. This record was then copied several times and circulated among officials and others who were interested. The original piece of papyrus or parchment recording the battle was lost, or simply fell to pieces. Some of the copies disappeared in the same way. Some survived.

The problem is – how can we tell whether the copies which

have survived until today are accurate copies of the original? The same procedure for answering this question applies whether the event is a battle, or a voyage, or a life – the life of Christ, for example.

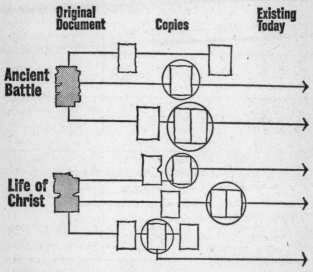

The manuscripts which have not been marked with a circle in the diagram have been lost, or worn out, or destroyed. We do not have the actual piece of papyrus on which Luke wrote his gospel, or the material on which Homer wrote his poetry, or the paper on which Shakespeare wrote his plays.

We can say that we possess an accurate record when (1) we possess several copies which are basically similar, and (2) the copies we have are fairly near in time to the original writer.

A time span which seems great to us will satisfy the experts, provided there are enough copies to enable them to cross-check. (Provided, also, that these copies were not all taken from the same copy. All copies will ultimately trace back to the original document, but to be really useful some of them must follow different lines on the previous diagram.)

Here is a table which compares the documents containing the life of Christ (i.e. the four Gospels) with some other famous ancient manuscripts.

Ancient Writing	Thucydides' HISTORY OF PELOPONNESIAN WAR	Caesar's GALLIC WAR	Tacitus' HISTORIES	The Four Gospels
(A) Original document written	430–400 BC	52–51 BC	AD 104–109	AD 65–90
(B) Oldest surviving copy	AD 900 (plus a few 1st Century fragments)	AD 850	AD 800	
(C) Approx. time between 'A' and 'B'	1300 years (Fragments 400 years)	900 years	700 years	
(D) Number of ancient copies in existence today	8	10	2	

In order to get the strength of the evidence for the Gospels, put your own estimates in the blank column in the diagram (we will consider 'D' first).

Obviously I would not suggest this if the evidence was not fairly impressive. Eight, ten and two copies for the other ancient documents. What then for the Gospels? Thirty? Fifty? Two hundred?

It proved difficult to find an accurate figure for the number of existing copies of the Gospels in Greek – the language in which they were originally written. To solve the problem I wrote to Tyndale House in Cambridge, for this is a centre which specializes in biblical research. They could not give me an accurate figure either, for the list is too long to count without taking a very long time! They suggested that I should use the phrase 'many hundreds, hundreds upon hundreds'. This figure is for copies which were made *before* AD 1000. The total rises to about 2,000 if we count later copies as well.

When we consider the rest of the New Testament, the figure rises to five thousand, provided we take into account those manuscripts which contain just a part. 'There are in existence about 5,000 Greek manuscripts of the New Testament in whole or part' writes Professor Bruce of Manchester University.

Parts are found because only a portion of some manuscripts survived, and because scribes sometimes copied only a section of the New Testament – Paul's letters or the Gospels for example. Start copying the 27 books of the New Testament and you will see why!

Now to the *time* factor. There are two copies of the New Testament – which of course, includes the Gospels – which are dated about AD 350, *less than three hundred years* after the original. This compares very favourably with the 1300, 900, and 700 years for other books. One of these very old copies of the New Testament is in the British Museum. It was bought by the British Government from the Soviet Government on Christmas Day 1933, for £100,000. The other is in the Vatican Library.

When we take smaller fragments into account the situation is even more impressive. A fragment of a copy of St John's Gospel was recently discovered in the sands of Egypt. It is dated by experts at approximately AD 130, which is only about fifty years after the original was written. It is now kept in the John Rylands Library in Manchester.

In view of this it is not surprising that Professor Bruce can write, 'there is much more evidence for the New Testament than for other ancient writings of comparable date'. Dr M. C. Tenney, an American scholar, adds his weight to this view, 'In spite of the numerous possibilities for error, the New

45

Testament is probably the most trustworthy piece of writing that has survived from antiquity'.

No one doubts that we have a reliable text of Caesar's *Gallic War* and the rest. The case for the reliability of the New Testament is far stronger.

The biblical archaeologist Sir Frederic Kenyon sums up the situation. 'Both the *authenticity* and the *general integrity* of the books of the New Testament may be regarded as finally established'.

We can be certain, then, that the copies of the New Testament which exist today are an accurate record of the original document which St Mark and the other evangelists wrote. But can we also be sure that these gospel writers recorded accurately the events concerning the life and death of Christ in the first place?

Could the writers have invented the material?
Jesus lived in the public eye from about AD 27 to AD 30, when He was crucified. The Gospels are very largely concerned with those three years.

Mark's Gospel was probably the first to be completed – in about AD 65. It is probable that large parts of Matthew and Luke – in particular those parts which record the teaching of Jesus – were written down by AD 50, some twenty years after the death of Jesus.

This seems a long time until we remember that the early Christians were much less concerned than we are with writing, as many people could not read, and much more concerned with speaking and memorizing. As a result their memories were much better trained than ours (Professor Nineham of Cambridge University, usually cautious on such matters, speaks of 'the wonderfully retentive memory of the Oriental' and maintains that we can 'often be virtually sure' that we have an accurate record of the deeds and words of Jesus).

46

The stories concerning Jesus were told from the moment He died. They were only written down when those who had been with Him during His life began to run the risk of death, either from persecution or from natural causes.

It was rather like a modern lecturer making a book out of the things which he had been saying in his lectures for several years. The items which are written in the Gospels are those things which had been preached about during the years following Christ's death. For example, we know from a man called Papias who was born in AD 60, that Mark used Peter's preaching as a basis for his Gospel.

A man who was 20 when Jesus was crucified would have been about 40 when the teaching material used by Matthew and Luke was written down and circulated, and about 55 when the same thing happened to Mark's Gospel.

Thousands had heard Jesus preach and seen Him in action. Thousands more had heard the teaching about Him from the time of His death. If one of the preachers had altered the account, or if the material when written down had been different from the preaching, there would have been an outcry – from friends *and* enemies.

The fact that there were plenty of eye-witnesses about does not guarantee every item in the Gospels, but it does guarantee their general reliability.

Winston Churchill did great things during the last war, but if someone now suggested that he had healed the sick or fed the crowds, the balloon would soon go up!

Another point is raised by the question, 'Could the writers have invented the teaching of Jesus?' Quite literally – Could they? Or are the sayings so great that only someone as great as Jesus could have uttered them.

Beverley Nichols made this point very forcibly some years ago.

'You cannot deny the reality of this character, *in whatever body it resided…somebody* said "The Sabbath was

47

made for man, and not man for the Sabbath"; *somebody* said "For what shall it profit a man if he shall gain the whole world and lose his own soul"; *somebody* said "Suffer the little children to come unto me, and forbid them not; for of such is the Kingdom of God"; *somebody* said "How hardly shall they that have riches enter into the Kingdom of God"; *somebody* said "All they that take the sword shall perish with the sword".

'*Somebody* said these things, because they are staring me in the face at this moment from the Bible. And whoever said them was *gigantic*. And whoever said them was *living*...we cannot find in any contemporary literature any phrases which have a shadow of the beauty, the truth, the individuality, nor the *indestructibility* of those phrases.

'And remember, I have only quoted five sentences at random' (*The Fool Hath Said*, Jonathan Cape).

Would the writers have invented the material?
Let us assume for a moment that it was possible for the Gospel writers to distort events or invent teaching which they attributed to Jesus. Even if they had the opportunity, would they have done so?

A good deal of the teaching in the Gospels is about morality – including honesty. Is it likely – or even possible – that some of the finest teaching about honesty which the world has ever known, is itself part of a huge lie?

Besides which, the sort of material which the Church leaders may have been tempted to make up is not included. For example, there was a tremendous argument in the Church at the time when the Gospels were being written, as to whether Gentile Christians should be made to keep the Jewish Law of circumcision.

If Jesus had said something about this, the matter would have been easily settled. But He didn't, and so the Gospels do not contain such teaching. An inventor – even a well-meaning one – would almost certainly have done so.

48

Can we check any of the details?
Yes we can. The science of archaeology continues to throw tremendous light upon the whole Bible. But this is such an important subject, that we will give it a short chapter to itself.

We have been studying historical evidence. Any historical 'proof' depends upon two things. First, the facts–documents, objects, eye-witness accounts, etc. Secondly, the willingness of the investigator to be open to the conclusions to which the facts point.

No one can take you to the Battle of Hastings. If you refuse to believe unless you see it for yourself, then you will never be convinced about anything in history, whether it is 1066, or the existence of Julius Caesar or Napoleon, or that the Great War began in 1914, or about Jesus Christ.

Some people refuse to be convinced no matter how strong the evidence. The Flat Earth Society maintains that pictures taken by Astronauts are clever fakes. 'The earth is flat,' they say. End of argument.

The evidence for Christianity is largely concerned with historical proof. All we Christians ask, is that the openness of mind which is necessary and proper for the study of history should not be withdrawn just for this particular aspect.

Books of interest

The New Testament Documents? Are they reliable? by F. F. Bruce (IVP)

Runaway World by Michael Green (IVP)

Ring of Truth by J. B. Phillips (Hodder and Stoughton)

CHAPTER SIX

What about the South Sea Scrolls?

The previous chapter mentioned archaeology. This chapter will look more closely at the importance of some of the many scrolls, tablets etc. which have been discovered in recent years.

The Dead Sea Scrolls

The question which forms the chapter heading was asked by a student. He had heard someone suggest that some scrolls had disproved the Bible, but could not remember the name!

He was, of course, referring to the Dead Sea Scrolls.

These were discovered in some caves near the Dead Sea, in 1947. They consist of several scrolls which were placed in the caves by a community of Jews which lived at Qumran (near Jerusalem, see the map) during the first centuries BC and AD.

The scrolls remained in the caves for 2,000 years, until they were discovered by an Arab boy who was looking for a lost goat.

They have achieved a fame far beyond most archaeological discoveries, because some writers have tried to use them as a basis for disproving Christianity. Professor Millar Burrows who was working in Palestine when the scrolls were discovered, opens his book *More Light on the Dead Sea Scrolls* with the remarkable statement that 'The Dead Sea Scrolls were discovered in America in the spring of 1955'. In case this seems to be a flat contradiction of the previous paragraph, perhaps I should quote his next line. 'They had been discovered in Palestine, of course, in 1947'.

The American and British public 'discovered' the scrolls then, because the writings of the literary critic Edmund Wilson were published in an influential American magazine in that year – and he maintained that the scrolls threw considerable doubts upon the origins of Christianity.

This theme was taken up by Mr John Allegro a British scholar who was working on the scrolls. He gave a talk on radio in 1956, in which he suggested that there were strong similarities between Jesus and the original leader of the community at Qumran. This man was called the Teacher of Righteousness, and he lived about 100 years before Jesus. Allegro inferred that Christ was not unique, and that the Christian gospel had its roots in the teaching of this Jewish sect which was flourishing before Jesus was born.

It is very important to notice that the views of Wilson and Allegro are shared by *very few other scholars*. Shortly after John Allegro's broadcast, a group consisting of members of the international team of experts working on the scrolls wrote to *The Times* in order to make it clear that they disagreed strongly with his views. Another letter in *The Times* (21 December, 1965) contained the sentence 'Nothing that appears in the scrolls hitherto discovered throws any doubt on the originality of Christianity'. It was signed by no less than eight university professors, who are experts in this field.

Professor Bruce, whose views on the New Testament were quoted in the last chapter, was Mr Allegro's head of department at Manchester University until the latter retired in 1970. He holds very different views from Allegro about the origins of Christianity as his books – including some on the Dead Sea Scrolls – show.

Most interesting of all, as Millar Burrows records in *More Light on the Dead Sea Scrolls*, John Allegro himself acknowledged that his views were drawn mainly from inference rather than evidence.

In May 1970 he published a book entitled *The Sacred Mushroom and the Cross* (followed in October by *End of a Road*). His May book was based largely upon philology (the science of language) and in it he argues that Christianity was started by the members of a fertility cult, whose main interests were drugs and sex. The New Testament, despite its obviously high moral tone, is in reality a code-book used by the cult, says Allegro.

His book was very well received by the *Sunday Mirror* which presented it in serial form. It was, however, very badly received by a number of experts, many of whom have done research in the same field.

On 26th May *The Times* published a letter signed by fifteen leading scholars, thirteen of whom were professors. They wrote:

'Sir – A good deal of publicity has recently been given to a book (*The Sacred Mushroom and the Cross*) by Mr John Allegro, formerly a lecturer at Manchester University.

'This is not a work upon which scholars would normally

wish to comment. But the undersigned, specialists in a number of relevant disciplines and men of several faiths and none, feel it their duty to let it be known that the book is not based on any philological or other evidence which they can regard as scholarly.

'In their view this work is an essay in fantasy rather than philology.

Yours etc. . .'

The sad thing is that while so many scholars feel that Allegro's views are demonstrably false, he still receives enormous publicity. *The Sacred Mushroom and the Cross* was widely reviewed in Africa as well as England and America, and was in its fourth edition within four months.

Far more people hear of his views than those of the very large number of scholars who strongly disagree with him. Some of the general public presumably conclude that Christianity has been finally debunked.

When a biblical scholar says 'I believe in Christ', no one is interested. When a biblical scholar says 'I don't believe in Christ', the newspapers are there like a flash. It is the old 'man bites dog' situation – only rather more serious.

If the Dead Sea Scrolls do not discredit Christianity, do they have any relevance to it at all?

Two things stand out. Firstly, they throw light upon the religious situation in the country of Jesus, during his life time. Anything which gives such information is obviously important for a clearer understanding of the New Testament, and of the life of Christ.

Secondly, they throw light upon the reliability of the text of parts of the Bible. At least part of every book in the Old Testament except one (Esther) has been found in the scrolls. The scrolls are in Hebrew – the language in which the Old Testament was originally written. They are much older than any other Hebrew Old Testament texts so far discovered – about one thousand years older in fact. Yet a comparison of those parts of the Bible found in the Dead Sea Scrolls with these other later copies shows a striking similarity. There *are* differences of course – several differences. This is inevitable with a time gap like this, and is no more alarming than the fact that the earliest copies of Shakespeare's plays show differences.

The really interesting thing is that the differences, though fairly frequent, do not affect the *sense*. If an American book is published in England, some changes may be made. Center will be changed to centre, cookie will be changed to biscuit, sidewalk will be changed to pavement. These are small details which will not alter the meaning. Many of the differences in these Bible texts are no bigger than these. Some of the other differences are accounted for by the usual, and almost unavoidable, errors made by scribes in the days before printing, when documents were copied by hand.

The *similarities* far outweigh the differences. The Dead Sea Scrolls have *increased* our confidence in the accuracy of the Bible.

Other discoveries

This tendency for archaeology to confirm the accuracy of the Bible is shown by several discoveries other than the Dead Sea Scrolls. A few examples are given below.

Until recently, we knew about Pontius Pilate the Roman governor only from the New Testament, and from the writings of Josephus the historian. In 1961 an Italian archaeological expedition working at Caesarea (about 65 miles from Jerusalem) discovered a stone slab, which was inscribed with three names including that of Pilate, and of the Emperor Tiberius.

In St John's Gospel (19.13) we read that Pilate judged Jesus at a place called the Pavement. In the 1930's Father

L. H. Vincent discovered a paved court covering 2,500 yards in Jerusalem at the Antonia Tower in the north-west corner of the Temple area. It is almost certainly the Pavement referred to in John.

In the *Acts of the Apostles* (18.12) we read that a man called Gallio was proconsul of Greece (sometimes called Achaia). A good deal is known about the movements of Gallio from his famous brother Seneca (who taught the Emperor Nero) and it seemed very difficult to fit in a spell as governor in Greece. Luke – who wrote *Acts* as well as the Gospel bearing his name – was thought to be wrong.

Recently an inscription was discovered which showed, not only that Gallio was proconsul, but the year during which he held this position – AD 51. This is just one of the very large number of details of *Acts* which have been proved correct.

Difficulties still remain. Not all the problems concerning people, places and dates of events in the Bible have been solved by archaeologists. There are still many points where our knowledge is incomplete or confused.

The fact remains that the list of discoveries which help clear up problems and vindicate the Bible at a purely factual level is very impressive.

Our last example is taken from the very first book in the Bible – the book of *Genesis*. The majority of *Genesis* is concerned with the Patriarchs – Abraham, Isaac, Jacob, etc.

These men lived as long before Christ as we live after.

Despite this very long time, discoveries made at Mari and Nuzu have thrown a great deal of light upon their customs, names and travels. (With the aid of the map and *Genesis* 11.31 – 12.10 you can trace the journey of Abraham via the area of these archaeological sites, into Egypt.)

So impressive is the evidence concerning these men, that Professor John Bright, an American scholar whose books are known to every student of theology, can say,

'We can assert with full confidence that Abraham, Isaac and Jacob were actual historical individuals'.

If we can speak with such certainty about the very first book of the Bible, and about men living two thousand years before Christ, it is clear that the Bible is very much more reliable than is often supposed.

In closing, a word of caution; archaeological evidence is *indirect* evidence. It shows us that the Bible is historically reliable. It gives us information about customs and places in Bible times. But it cannot directly prove or disprove the truth of Christianity. And it certainly cannot prove or disprove the existence of God.

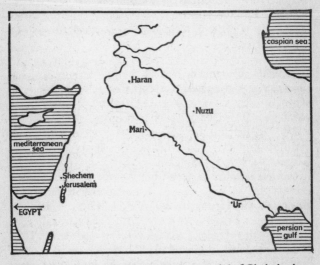

What it *does* show is that the basic material of Christianity – the Bible – is reliable, and this is a very important first step.

Concluding quotations

We will let the experts themselves have the last word.

'It is my considered conclusion, however, that if one will go through any of the historic statements of Christian faith he will find nothing that has been or can be disproved by the Dead Sea Scrolls' – Professor Millar Burrows (Yale University)

'As is the case also with the Old Testament, the work of the archaeologist has done much to...confirm the general witness of the early Church to the authentic nature of primitive (i.e. early) Christianity' – Professor R. K. Harrison (University of Toronto)

'Thus archaeological discovery has, at point after point, tended to confirm John's topography, even if all problems have not been finally solved' – Professor A. M. Hunter (University of Aberdeen)

'...it is a fact that, by and large, modern archaeological science has done a great deal to confirm the accuracy of the history recorded in the Bible, and only rarely and in relatively unimportant matters does it put a question mark against the biblical record' – Dr I. H. Marshall (University of Aberdeen)

'...it may be stated categorically that no archaeological discovery has ever controverted a biblical reference' – Dr Nelson Glueck (President of the Hebrew Union College Biblical and Archaeological School)

Books of interest

Archaeology of the Old Testament by R. K. Harrison (Hodder and Stoughton)

Archaeology of the New Testament by R. K. Harrison (Hodder and Stoughton)

Both books contain material on the Dead Sea Scrolls, as well as other archaeological finds.

CHAPTER SEVEN

Why Does God Allow Suffering?

Every day hundreds of thousands of animals are eaten by other animals. Every year there are natural disasters.

On Sunday, 31 May 1970, a terrible earthquake shook Peru. Tens of thousands were killed. This followed a series of disasters which marked the new decade. Avalanches in Switzerland, an earthquake in Turkey, floods in Rumania. Each of these was a killer.

Christ's grim words have again been grimly fulfilled, 'For nation will make war upon nation, kingdom upon kingdom; there will be famines and earthquakes in many places' (Matthew 24.7).

In Britain the small Welsh town of Aberfan is still a

household name. Welshmen will never forget that terrible day in October 1966, when 144 people were killed when a huge mountain of coal waste collapsed. 116 of them were children.

Why did God allow these things to happen?

As we consider this question we are faced with the most difficult problem which can confront a person who believes in a loving and powerful God. Is there an answer?

Certainly there is no *easy* answer, but this does not mean that we can say nothing. As we consider the problem it becomes clear that the fact of suffering raises, not one, but two, questions for the Christian.

Question One – Why does God allow these things to happen?
Question Two – Does God really care for mankind? Indeed, is He really there at all?

We will look at each of these in turn.

Why?

Why does God allow such things to happen?

The short answer is – we simply do not know. When we consider why a particular accident happened, or why a child died at such an early age, we are forced to admit that we can give no answer.

We find important *clues* in the Bible. We read in the book of Genesis that man rebelled against God, and that this affected the world in which man lived.

The *ultimate* answer to the problem of suffering is to be found along these lines but our investigations will not take us that far. Our problem is more immediate. Why *this* earthquake? Why *that* accident?

Reluctantly we admit that, usually, we can give no answer.

We need to remember, however, that to say that we do not know the reason, is quite different from saying that there is no reason. When my television set went wrong recently, I had no idea why it gave a thin bright band instead of a picture. But I was quite sure that a reason existed, and this is why I sent for a television engineer.

Does God care?

Behind the question *why*, stands this further question. We have an uneasy feeling that the God who allows these things to happen may not really care for us after all.

Does God care? Does God love the world which He has created? Here we *can* give a clear and definite answer, for we have clear and definite evidence. Yes, God *does* love us. We know this because He has given us a clear demonstration of His love. He sent His Son to die for us.

This may seem at first sight a slick and disappointing answer. It is in fact the greatest of all answers to the greatest of all questions. It is the keynote of the New Testament. Does God love the world? Says St John, 'God loved the world so much that He gave His only Son' (John 3. 16).

Here, as always, it is the fact of Christ which makes sense of life. The fact of Christ is *the answer* to the problem of suffering.

The balance principle

Very often life demands that we 'weigh' facts.

A friend is accused of theft. There is evidence which appears to be against him. He was outside the supermarket with some items in his bag.

What can we put on the other side of the balance? We *know* our friend. All our experience of him suggests that he is honest. We know that when he found a £5 note on one occasion he handed it to the police.

The fact that he was found with the goods presents a problem for our faith in our friend. We balance against this evidence the fact of our knowledge of him. We then decide which way the balance must come down.

Of course, we may suspect that our friend is basically dishonest, in which case there is nothing we can put on the right-hand side. It is not the details which matter here, but the way in which we tackle a problem like this.

This balance principle provides the key to the solution of the problem which pain and suffering present to our belief in God.

We must insist on looking at *all* of the evidence. The atheist will draw our attention to part of the evidence – the fact of suffering. We must take this into account. Certainly it weighs heavily on the left-hand side of the balance.

But we must also take into account the fact of Jesus Christ, for this too is evidence. If it is true that God sent His Son because He loves us, then this tips the scales.

Two further illustrations will make the issues clearer.

A war story

Imagine the following situation during the last war. Mr Brown was involved with the French Underground

Resistance against the Nazis. He was introduced to M. Defarge who, he was told, was the head of the Resistance Movement. They worked together and Mr Brown was tremendously impressed with M. Defarge.

On one occasion they planned to blow up an ammunition store. It was almost certain that those who took part would be killed. Defarge's son volunteered, and with much grief Defarge allowed him to go. The mission was successful but his son was killed.

One day, Defarge told Brown that they must alter their tactics. He warned Brown that he would see him doing things which he would not understand.

On occasions, Brown saw Defarge helping their own men to escape. On other occasions Brown saw him standing by while their men were handed over to the Nazis. Sometimes Defarge even appeared in the uniform of the enemy. 'He is a traitor!' cried Brown's comrades.

But Brown knew Defarge. In particular, he knew that he had allowed his son to die for the cause. He knew that he could be trusted. He was often bewildered, but he knew that although he could not understand, there must be a reason.

At last, the war was over. Brown and Defarge met once more, and Defarge explained why he did those things which at the time were so bewildering.

The atheist is in the position of Brown's comrades. He considers only part of the evidence – the fact of suffering.

The Christian is like Brown. He is often bewildered by events which he cannot understand. His faith is sorely tried by events which suggest that God does not care.

But he knows God. Above all he knows that God sent His Son to die for us. It is because of this that he is certain that God loves us.

An incident from the mission field

This time we are dealing with fact. John Paton was a Christian missionary. In 1858 he and his young pregnant wife went to the primitive Island of Tanna in the New Hebrides.

During the first year she died of fever. This was followed 17 days later by the death of his one-month old son.

Grief stricken, John Paton buried his wife and child.

He recorded these words:

'It was very difficult to be resigned, left alone, and in sorrowful circumstances; but feeling immovably assured that my God and Father was too wise and loving to err in anything that He does or permits, I looked up to the Lord for help, and struggled on in His work. I do not pretend to see through the mystery of such visitations – wherein God calls away the young, the promising, and those sorely needed for His service here; but this I do know and feel, that, in the light of such dispensations, it becomes us all to love and serve our blessed Lord Jesus so that we may be ready at His call for death and Eternity' (James Paton: *The Story of John G. Paton*, Hodder).

Notice: 'I do not pretend to see through the mystery...' To the question *why* he could give no answer.

But he did not stop at that. To our second question, he affirmed that *God is a Father who loves*.

This is the authentic voice of faith. The man with a living faith is often bewildered, but *he is prepared to live with questions which he cannot answer, in the light of the great answers which he* does *possess*.

Such faith is not a blind refusal to face the facts. Rather, it comes from a concern to take into account *all* the facts – the fact of suffering *and* the fact of Christ. Such faith is not based on a refusal to consider the evidence; indeed it springs from a refusal to leave out that part of the evidence which non-Christians so often ignore – the evidence of God's love shown clearly by the fact that He sent His Son.

But all this raises another big question. Is the coming of

Jesus Christ into our world a fact of sufficient importance to weigh down the scales? Clearly the whole solution depends on this.

Is Jesus *that* significant. We turn to this question in our next chapter.

Books of interest

The Mountain That Moved by Edward England (Hodder and Stoughton) The story of Aberfan

The Problem of Pain by C. S. Lewis (Fontana)

Miracle on the River Kwai by E. Gordon (Fontana)

Tortured for Christ by R. Wurmbrand (Hodder and Stoughton)

Through Gates of Splendour by E. Elliot (Hodder and Stoughton)

Taught by Pain by Mary Endersbee (Falcon)

CHAPTER EIGHT

Jesus, Buddha, Muhammad— What's the difference?

The person of Christ

Christianity is based, not only on ideas, but on events. At its centre we do not find a theory, but a person – the person of Jesus Christ.

He is a person who is widely misunderstood. Very many people have a false mental picture of Him, stemming perhaps from a certain type of religious art, or from a failure to grow up from Sunday School thinking. Far too often Jesus seems to be thought of as a rather anaemic character, more interested in flowers, birds and children than in the harsh adult world of reality.

How different is the towering figure of the New Testament! We see there a man marked out as a dangerous rebel by the corrupt authorities of His day; a man who drew tremendous crowds; a man who inspired others to deeds of heroism; a man who took the uncompromising road to martyrdom; a man who knew a wide range of human emotions and problems – sadness, anger, disappointment, hunger, thirst, and agonizing pain.

Christ was interested in children of course, but He was also a man among men, and the world He moved in was largely a man's world – a harsh world of hatred, intrigue, brutality, and revenge.

The Gospels show us a dynamic figure who waged war against evil with the weapons of love, openness, kindness, and forgiveness.

Not that He was soft. Against those greatest evils of pride, hypocrisy and humbug His attack was blistering and devastating.

Men fitting the above description are rare. But not unique, perhaps. A fair number of men have shown at least some of these qualities. And a few men have demonstrated sufficient dynamic to found great religious movements – Gautama the Buddha who founded Buddhism, and Muhammad the founder of the Muslim religion for example.

Why should we follow Christ and Christianity, rather than the Buddha and Buddhism or Muhammad and Islam? These too were great men. Is there any real difference between them?

The teaching of Christ

One really big difference is found in Christ's *teaching*. Not in His teaching about morality or religion, but in His teaching about *Himself*. When we study Christ's view of Himself and His mission, and His sense of His own authority, we find something unique.

66

In St John's Gospel, we read that the Jewish leaders were determined to kill Jesus, 'because...he claimed equality with God' (John 5. 18). It is this staggering claim which is unique among the great religious teachers of the world. It is a claim which occurs many times and in many ways throughout the Gospels. Here are three examples from the mass of available material.

Titles
He referred to Himself by names reserved for God in the Old Testament. The word 'Lord' in the Bible sometimes means simply 'Master' or 'Sir'. Very often however it is a title for God and sometimes Jesus used the title about Himself in this sense. An example can be seen at the end of the Sermon on the Mount (Matthew 7. 21–23).

On another occasion Jesus said, 'before Abraham was born, I am' (John 8. 58). This sounds like bad grammar until we realize that 'I am' was the title by which God had identified Himself to Moses at the burning bush (Exodus 3. 14). Jesus was claiming to be God by using this title, and the Jewish leaders who were arguing with him knew it. As a result they tried to stone Him, for stoning was the penalty for blasphemy.

Judgment
In various passages, such as the Parable of the Sheep and the Goats (Matthew 25. 31–46), Jesus spoke about man's final destiny. He calmly assumed that it was He, Jesus, who would act as Judge of the world, at the end of time.

When we recall that those to whom He was speaking recognized only God as the Judge of mankind, we see just how far-reaching was the claim which Jesus was making.

Worship
When the disciples worshipped Him (Matthew 14. 33) and

when Thomas fell down before him saying 'My Lord and my God!' (John 20. 28), Jesus calmly accepted their worship. The tremendous difference between His attitude and that of the apostles when men wanted to worship them can be seen in Acts 14. 8-18. Paul and Barnabas were horrified when the men at Lystra tried to worship them. They knew that only God was to be worshipped, and that for men to accept worship was blasphemy.

The stark alternatives are beginning to emerge. Either Jesus was blaspheming – or He was God. But before developing this point it is worth pausing to consider why it is that although this sort of teaching is so widespread in the Gospels, it is so easily missed. People are often surprised when it is pointed out to them – even when they know the Gospels fairly well.

Very probably, part of the reason is that Jesus' teaching about Himself is often found in the course of His other teaching. He underlines His teaching about behaviour, or the Kingdom of God, or anxiety and so on by reminding His hearers that He has a unique authority to speak on these matters.

It seems so natural, that we miss its force.

Great men don't need to boast, but they don't need to adopt an attitude of unreal humility either. When Rod Laver says in a television interview, 'I'm playing good tennis at the moment', he is not being conceited. He is simply speaking the truth, and in the light of this, assessing his chances of winning Wimbledon.

In the same sort of way, Jesus, with no trace of conceit, says, 'I am the light of the world', 'I am the way, the truth and the life', and 'Come to me, all whose work is hard, whose load is heavy; and I will give you relief' (John 9.5; 14. 6; Matthew 11. 28).

But I suspect that the main reason this teaching is often overlooked is that it is the very last thing we expect to find.

68

We know that Jesus taught the need for humility by associating with, and serving, ordinary people. He chose working men for His close companions. He lived a simple rough life, and was prepared to befriend social outcasts.

To find such a humble man saying the sort of things which Jesus said about Himself is puzzling – even shocking.

It is vitally important to realize that Jesus alone among the founders of the great religions of the world, spoke in this way. Muhammad and the Buddha claimed to be *messengers* of the Truth. Muhammad was the 'Prophet of God'. Gautama became 'the Enlightened One' (this is what the word 'Buddha' means). They felt that they had a deeper insight into the Truth than most other men, and it was this insight which they wished to pass on.

Jesus claimed to be the very *source of Truth*. There is all the difference between these two attitudes.

Followers of other religions are as anxious to make clear this difference as Christians are. The English Buddhist Maurice Walsh has pointed out that the Buddhist view of Buddha is very different from the Christian view of Christ. He stressed that the Buddha is thought of as a Teacher–*not* a Saviour.

The same approach applies within Islam. Dr E. G. Parrinder has made the point that Muslims 'do not like the title Muhammadan', because 'they do not worship Muhammad but they believe that he was the last and greatest Apostle of God'. How different is Christianity! Christians glory that their name identifies them closely with Christ, whom they reverence as Teacher, Saviour and God.

Was Jesus right?

And so to the really big question. It is one thing to say the things which Jesus said. But were they true?

Notice that I have said that none of the other founders of

the great religions of the world have thought of themselves as Jesus did. But I have not said that *no* other men have thought in this way.

Some rulers have claimed to be divine. Herod Agrippa I for example (see Acts 12. 19–24 for details) and some of the Roman Emperors. Such rulers were usually proud, arrogant men. Even so, their claims were less far-reaching than those of Jesus. They lived in societies which believed in several gods. Jesus and His fellow countrymen believed in One God.

Even in modern times we occasionally find men who hold similar views about themselves. We meet them, if at all, in homes for the mentally unbalanced.

It is as simple as that. Only three kinds of men could make such claims. An extremely unbalanced person who had great but false ideas about his own greatness; a liar who wanted to impress people, or the One Person of whom those claims are true.

There is no fourth possibility. We cannot deny that Jesus was God, and in the next breath speak of Him as a good man and a great teacher. If we refuse to accept His own estimate of Himself, the alternatives are much harder than this.

He would not be a good man if He made these claims knowing them to be untrue. And He would not be a great teacher if He was wrong on this fundamental aspect of His teaching – even if He sincerely believed what he was saying.

Either we accept that Jesus was God or we number Him with the world's lunatics or liars. Ordinary, sane and moral men do not speak about themselves as Jesus spoke.

It is as clear cut as this. Was Jesus insane – falsely believing Himself to be Divine? Was He an impostor – merely pretending to be God? Or was He who He claimed to be?

We can easily make sense of the Buddha – He was a good, great man. We can easily make sense of Muhammad – he was a dynamic leader of men. We can easily make sense of Confucius – he was a very wise teacher. We cannot make sense of Christ at all – unless He was God; or mad.

The solution

The only way to decide this question is to examine His behaviour. Does His character measure up to His claims or was this just 'big-talk'.

Those who lived at the time of Jesus watched Him closely. Several of them came to the conclusion that His claims, incredible as they were, were in fact true. They were forced to this decision by the sheer quality of His life – by the combination of sanity, wisdom, strength and transparent goodness.

Some of these were members of the party which opposed Jesus and they had a lot to lose. Nicodemus and Joseph of Arimathaea for example. And it probably wasn't too good for the military career of the Roman Centurion to declare 'Beyond all doubt, this man was innocent' (Luke 23.47).

Others knew Him so well and for so long that they would have seen through a lie or a bluff. After three years of very close acquaintance with Jesus, Peter could write 'He committed no sin' (1. Peter 2 22). We find the same thought in John's first letter – 'there is no sin in Him' (1 John 3. 5).

We too can examine His character – by reading the Gospels (Mark's Gospel is probably the best starting point). The issues are far too important to ignore or shelve. If Jesus Christ really is divine; if God really has come to the world in the person of Jesus Christ; if we really are a 'visited planet'... If these things are true they stagger the imagination. And the practical implications are enormous.

They demand that we give to Christ our obedience and worship. We are bound to revise our whole outlook on life in the light of what He said and did.

Concluding quotations

'The historical difficulty of giving for the life, sayings and influence of Jesus any explanation that is not harder than the Christian explanation, is very great' – Professor C. S. Lewis (Cambridge University).

'No mortal man makes such a claim, or we know him to be mad. We are driven back on the words of wise old "Rabbi" Duncan: "Christ either deceived mankind by conscious fraud, or He was Himself deluded, or He was divine. There is no getting out of this trilemma."

'Christians have never been in any doubt which of these propositions is true' – Professor A. M. Hunter (Aberdeen University).

Books of interest

Mere Christianity by C. S. Lewis (Fontana); especially the chapter entitled 'The Shocking Alternative'

My God is Real by D. C. K. Watson (Falcon)

CHAPTER NINE

Once dead, always dead

Hugh Anderson died on 12 August, 1970. He was 21. He had cancer – and knew it.

He packed a great deal into those 21 years. He had been president of the Cambridge University Union, and he was a brilliant debater. He was deeply interested in politics, and his concern for social justice led him, during the summer holiday of 1969, to organize a project to help immigrant children to speak English.

His father, Professor J. N. D. Anderson, is Director of the Institute of Advanced Legal Studies in the University of London. He is also a well-known Christian, and five days after the death of his son, he gave the 'Thought for the day' radio talk.

His subject was the resurrection of Christ.

After giving the reasons why he is convinced about the fact of the Resurrection, he continued: 'On this I am prepared to stake my life. In this faith my son died, after saying, "I'm going to my Lord". I am convinced that he was not mistaken.'

They both understood the vast implications of Christ's resurrection. If it is true, then death is not the end but a new and glorious beginning. Life has real meaning after all.

In this chapter we look at some of the evidence which convinced those two highly intelligent men.

Nobody saw the Resurrection happen. There were people on the spot very soon afterwards, but no one was actually there when Christ rose. We are, of course, well accustomed to this sort of situation – the police handle problems like this every day.

Sorting out whether Christ rose from the dead or not, is rather like a murder case. But in reverse.

The police discover a body. No one saw the murder take place, but certain other related facts come to light – the fact that Jones was jealous of the victim; the fact that a blood-stained iron bar was found nearby; the fact that White's finger prints were on the wallet...

The detectives, and then the lawyers and the jury, try to discover the most likely explanation for these facts. The case is decided if the explanation for each of the facts, or clues, points in the same direction.

So it is with Christ's resurrection, except that the problem is reversed. We are dealing, not with someone said to be murdered, but with someone said to have come alive from the dead.

No one saw what happened to the body. But certain other related facts came to light – facts which demand an explanation just as much as the blood and the finger prints in the murder case.

We shall examine five such facts, and try to find the most likely explanation for each of them.

First Fact: The impact of Christ on the world

Only a handful of men have founded great movements, and made a really decisive impact on history. Each of these men has needed time in which to make his influence felt. Each of them, that is, except Jesus Christ. Here are some significant details about some of the great men who have gained a huge number of followers:

Confucius: (The great Chinese Teacher)
   Died in 479 BC, aged 72
Gautama the Buddha: (Founder of Buddhism)
   Died in 483 BC, aged 80
Muhammad: (Founder of the Muslim Religion)
   Died in AD 632, aged 62
Karl Marx: (The great mind behind Communism)
   Died in 1883, aged 64

Now compare and *contrast* Jesus Christ. He died in AD 30, as a young man in His thirties. He spent *only three years* in the public eye, and even these years were spent in a fairly remote place. When He died he left no writing, and only a few dispirited, demoralized followers.

Yet Christ's impact on history has been just as great, and probably greater, than those listed above. This village carpenter is now so famous that we don't set aside one day in the year to remember Him by, as we do with many other great men; we base our whole calendar on His life. Every time we write the date we pay an unconscious tribute to the birth of Christ. The essayist R. W. Emerson could say that the name of Jesus 'is not so much written as ploughed into the history of the world'.

This is a fact which demands an explanation. How could Christ make such an impact in such a short time?

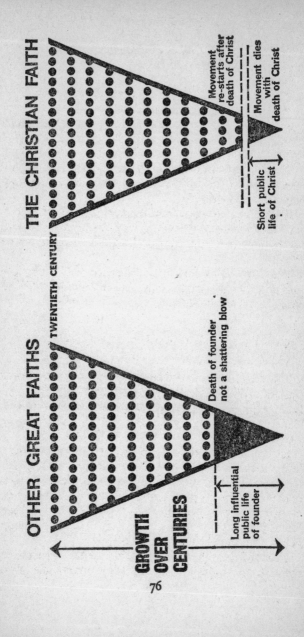

OTHER GREAT FAITHS

GROWTH OVER CENTURIES

Long influential public life of founder

Death of founder not a shattering blow

TWENTIETH CENTURY

THE CHRISTIAN FAITH

Movement re-starts after death of Christ

Movement dies with death of Christ

Short public life of Christ

It is clear that His influence continued for more – much more – than three years.

But how?

Men continue to influence the world after they are dead by their writings, or through their followers.

But Jesus left no writing. And the impact of His short earthly life on His disciples was largely cancelled by the shattering blow caused by His early death.

The only satisfactory answer is given in the New Testament – Jesus Himself lived on and continued to exert an influence, after His death.

If Jesus had not risen from the grave, His death would have been mourned by His relatively few friends, and His family. Within two generations He would have been forgotten.

The only really satisfactory explanation for Christ's impact on the world, considering His brief life, is that God raised Him from the dead.

Second Fact: Several people claimed that they saw the risen Christ

St Paul wrote a letter to the Christians in the Greek town of Corinth about 25 years after the death of Christ. In this letter he gave a list of people who claimed that they saw Christ, alive and well, after His death on the cross (see 1 Corinthians 15).

James was one. Peter was another. These men also wrote letters which are in the New Testament, and their letters, together with other information, show that they were men of the very highest moral calibre. We can be quite certain of their honesty. When they said they had seen Jesus, they meant it – and were prepared to suffer and die for their belief. They were as certain as that.

Then there was the group of five hundred. Paul reminded the Corinthians that most of these were still alive when he wrote. Their testimony could easily be checked.

A clergyman in Ipswich one Easter Sunday, came down from the pulpit, took off his jacket, and stood on his head. When young Willy Smith was asked by his mother what the sermon was about, she could be excused for scolding him (or even clipping his ear!) for telling stories.

It *was* an unusual event. We do not easily accept the word of one person for something like that. But if several people claim that they saw the same thing, including several older members of the Church who are known to be honest – what then? We would be forced to accept their word about that headstand.

We are right to view a report that someone has risen from the dead with suspicion. But if enough people claim to have seen him, and if other evidence points in the same direction, a refusal to believe is not to display a healthy suspicion of an unusual happening. It is to display a point-blank refusal to face facts.

Third Fact: The disciples were transformed

Christianity began very differently from any other great world movement. Every other movement – Islam, Buddhism, Communism etc – has swung into action during the lifetime of its Founder, and has either been well under way by the time of the Founder's death, or has been put on the map later by a group of equally able men who picked up where he left off.

The death of Karl Marx, for example, did not come as a crushing blow to the Communist movement. When he died he left a great deal of writing, and some very able dedicated followers, who built on his foundations.

Although Communism was not a world movement when he died in London in 1883, it does not surprise us to discover that Lenin and the others who followed Marx were able to translate his ideas into a dynamic movement. Marx, Engels,

Lenin and their comrades, really looked like men who might start something big.

It was not so with Christ and the Apostles. As we read the Gospels it looks for a while as if Jesus is going to fit into the same pattern. He was at one time a popular leader with a large following, and it would be easy to understand the existence of the Church if it had grown steadily as a result of His dynamic teaching.

There would be no problem if, when He died, He had left a large group of followers, including a smaller circle of able, convinced leaders.

But the story does not run like that. There was an ugly break. After appearing in public for only three years He was rejected by the crowd and put to death by the leaders. The popular preacher was abruptly silenced. The thousands who followed Him melted away without offering any resistance, or actually turned against Him. Even those who remained loyal were disillusioned. His inner circle of followers deserted Him at the end, when the pressure was really on. The leader of this group even denied all knowledge of Him.

If the movement which He started was to continue, these were the men who must take the lead. But even though they reassembled after His death they showed no signs of carrying on where He left off. They were thoroughly frightened and disillusioned – not a very promising start.

To sum up: The Church almost did not begin at all. It almost came to an abrupt end when Christ was put to death. It looked as if yet another Jewish revolution had fizzled out.

But of course, it didn't work out that way. The whole thing started up again. It restarted shortly after the death of Christ, when those who had been crushed and shattered by the crucifixion of their leader, suddenly began preaching that God had raised Him from the dead.

The small group of men which Christ left behind wasn't likely to start anything – except perhaps a fishing business.

They certainly weren't likely candidates for starting a movement which would sweep the world. Yet they did just that.

One thing is clear. Before they could do this they needed to be transformed. The New Testament tells us that this is just what did happen. Shortly after Christ's death, they *were* transformed. In place of bitter disappointment there was joyful certainty; in place of fear there was boldness; instead of hiding behind locked doors, they were out preaching to the crowds; instead of thinking gloomily that their leader was dead, they proclaimed that He had conquered death.

Peter the coward who had denied Christ, became Peter the Rock who fearlessly preached in front of the very people who had executed Jesus.

That the disciples were transformed is a fact. How can it be accounted for?

Recently, I heard a man who was for many years a high-ranking pilot in the RAF give his views on this. He is now a Christian minister, and he was explaining how he became a convinced Christian in the first place.

He was recovering from 'flu, and having nothing much to read he picked up a copy of the New English Bible New Testament which his wife had bought. He began to read, and it gripped him. He put the Bible down in the early hours of the morning. One thing had become clear to him – the resurrection of Christ was a fact. He knew that this was the only possible explanation for the incredible change which took place in the disciples.

He was an experienced leader of men. During the war he was awarded the Distinguished Flying Cross and he had been a prisoner under the Japanese. He understood how men behave under stress.

He knew that men do not reassemble and organize themselves effectively after the sort of crushing disappointment which Christ's disciples had experienced.

A handful of frightened men would not suddenly preach boldly to the very people who had killed their leader – and so risk their own lives. Men just do not behave like that – *unless* something tremendous happens to drive away the bitter disappointment. That Wing Commander became convinced that in the case of the disciples, that necessary 'something' must have happened. Christ really must have appeared to them after rising from the dead.

He realized – without anyone pointing it out to him – that this was the only possible explanation for the disciples' subsequent behaviour. That discovery set in motion the process which was to revolutionize his life.

When we read of a satellite circling the earth, we know that it was not the explosion of a child's firework which put it there. A big fact requires a big explanation.

The same is true here. The startling transformation in the disciples, and the beginning of the Church which sprang from this, are 'big' facts. They require a sufficiently 'big' explanation.

The only really adequate explanation is the one given in the New Testament – Christ conquered death, and appeared to His disciples. When He finally left them, He sent His Spirit to be with them.

Professor C. F. D. Moule of Cambridge puts it like this: 'If the coming into existence of the Nazarenes (i.e. the Christian Church) ...rips a great hole in history, a hole of the size and shape of resurrection, what does the secular historian propose to stop it up with?'

Fourth Fact: The body disappeared

After the crucifixion, the body of Jesus was wrapped in grave-clothes, and laid in a tomb belonging to Joseph of Arimathea. This happened on Good Friday.

On Easter Sunday, the body had disappeared, although the grave-clothes had been left behind in the tomb.

It wasn't the work of *thieves*. They could not have got past the guard, and they certainly would not have left the grave-clothes behind.

It could not have been the *disciples* who had taken the body, either. Not just because of the guard, but for a much more significant reason.

If the disciples had stolen the body, their bold preaching that Christ had risen from the dead would have been a lie. This preaching caused them a great deal of trouble and suffering, and for some it meant death.

Men are prepared to suffer for something they believe in passionately. No man is prepared to suffer for something he knows to be untrue. We tell lies to get *out* of trouble, not to get *into* it.

This leaves the *authorities*. Did they take the body? This explanation doesn't fit either.

Notice that the Church began, not primarily by the spreading of ideas, but by the proclaiming of a fact. Something had *happened*, said the Apostles – Christ had risen from the dead.

To disprove an idea you must argue. To disprove a fact, you must produce evidence. Those who wanted to discredit the Apostles – and the Jewish leaders wanted to do that very much indeed – had only to produce one piece of evidence to make the disciples look completely ridiculous.

All they had to do was to produce the body of Jesus. *If they had done that we would never have heard of Him or His followers. There would be no Church.*

It is very significant that they could not do this. If the authorities had taken the body, or discovered it still in the tomb, they would simply have produced it when Peter and the rest began preaching that Christ had risen. Instead, they imprisoned, threatened, and beat the Apostles.

It is absolutely certain that the authorities had no idea at all what had happened to Jesus. Yet the stubborn fact remains – His body had gone.

The Christian explanation seems to be the only alternative. Christ *did* rise from the dead.

Fifth Fact: Christ's power today

The evidence is not confined to the past. Thousands of men and women have experienced, and continue to experience, a new power in their lives. Although of differing backgrounds, ages and temperament, they put it down to the same cause – the power of the risen Christ working in their lives today.

Ted Dexter, the England Test Cricketer who now commentates on BBC Television, is an interesting example. He admits that until recently he was a compulsive gambler. This was having a very bad effect on his own life and that of his family, but he just could not master his desire to back horses. He found the moral power he needed to fight this problem when he became a Christian.

To put it another way – he met the living, risen Christ.

Conclusion

On the back seat of my car there is a doll. This is a fact which invites an explanation.

Someone might say: 'I can explain that doll. The man who owns the car is an eccentric parson who plays with dolls.' Someone else might disagree. 'No, he is not eccentric. He is a serious doll-collector. Some people collect stamps. Others collect coins. He collects dolls.'

Someone else – especially someone who knows me – might say: 'No, he has a small daughter. She probably left the doll in the car.'

That is by far the most likely explanation, and it is in fact the correct one.

It is my contention that the resurrection of Jesus from the dead is as superior to all other explanations for the facts we have been thinking about, as that last explanation about the doll.

We have been sifting evidence, so we will let a lawyer have the last word. Sir Edward Clarke KC, wrote:

'As a lawyer I have made a prolonged study of the evidences for the events of the first Easter Day. To me the evidence is conclusive, and over and over again in the High Court I have secured the verdict on evidence not nearly so compelling.'

Books of interest

The Evidence for The Resurrection by J. N. D. Anderson (IVP)

Christianity: the witness of history by J. N. D. Anderson (IVP)

Man Alive by Michael Green (IVP)

CHAPTER TEN

Prove it!

Does God exist? This apparently abstract question can be very practical. A young married woman wrote to *The Times* in 1970 with a problem. In her letter she asked whether she and her husband should remain faithful to each other, in order to provide a strong family unit in which her children could grow up. It was a serious question. Would the couple find a greater fulfilment by following the teaching of some modern thinkers, and having sexual relationships with a variety of other people?

If that woman believed that God exists, and that He has given us certain laws for our guidance and obedience – including the commandment 'You shall not commit adultery' (Exodus 20. 14) – she would find an answer to her very practical question.

A man who is now an alcoholic and a tramp said that his downward slide began as a result of a feeling of guilt after becoming father to his girlfriend's baby as a young man. If he believed that God exists and that He is forgiving and merciful, that man's life would be very different indeed.

No opting out

There is in fact no opting out of belief. Faith is not a question of believing a hundred impossible things before breakfast. Christians are called 'believers', but all men base their lives on assumptions which cannot be proved with mathematical certainty. The Christian *believes* that God exists. The Atheist *believes* that God does not exist. The Agnostic *believes* that there is not sufficient evidence to decide one way or the other. The indifferent person *believes* that it does not matter either way.

It is not a question of *whether* we believe but *what* we believe – and whether our beliefs are backed up by the available evidence. For not all acts of faith are equally likely to be true.

Bookmakers base their whole lives on the fact that some acts of faith have more evidence to support them than others. That is why some horses run at 100–1 and others are odds on favourites.

What about belief in God? Is there any evidence to support this act of faith? Many reasons for this belief have been given during the history of mankind. From this mass of ideas, we will single out and examine three particularly important reasons.

Design in the universe

We see the marks of design in the universe. Where there is design, there must be a Designer. We call that Designer God.

This sums up the famous Argument from Design (called the Teleological Argument by philosophers). We will examine the two parts of the argument separately.

(1) *Is there evidence of design?*

A woman looked through a microscope. What she saw was so beautiful that she thought it was a diamond. In fact she was looking at the eye of a water-flea.

We find design and beauty even in the smallest things.

But of course, it can be argued that things like eyes are the result of thousands of years of adaptation to the environment. And so another form of this argument has been put forward, which concentrates on those things which *cannot* adapt.

A large number of factors in our world are just right to support life. If the earth was much smaller there would be insufficient force of gravity to hold air around our planet. If the moon was much nearer or much bigger, there would be massive tidal waves, caused by its gravitational pull. If we were nearer the sun we would fry. If we were further away we would freeze.

In fact, of course, there would be no 'we'. It is sometimes argued that if these factors were different, there would be life on our planet, but of a different sort. But if some of these things did not apply, there would be no life at all – nothing can live without an atmosphere for example.

Another factor which is 'just right' is water. This substance, which is so common that we take it for granted, has some very remarkable properties indeed. It dissolves a very large number of substances – probably more than any other liquid (in the blood it holds in solution at least 64 substances). It is not easily decomposed. It boils and freezes at temperatures which are ideally suited to the temperature range of our planet.

Most interesting of all are its almost unique properties when it nears its freezing point. Fill a vessel with almost any liquid, and cool it below its freezing point. It will go solid at the bottom first. Except water. Almost alone among thousands of fluids, water freezes at the *surface* instead.

This occurs because water expands on freezing, while

other fluids contract. It is a vital property, for creatures which live in water would be killed when the temperature fell below freezing point for any appreciable time, if this did not happen, as lakes would freeze solid. This property is also important for the production of soil (and hence vegetation) because the expanding action of water as it freezes breaks up rocks. It is less good for lead water-pipes, for the same reason!

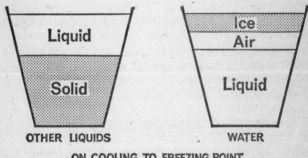

ON COOLING TO FREEZING POINT

Clearly then, there are marks of design and order in our universe. This is not to say that *all* is beauty, harmony and order, of course. We have already noted the fact of disharmony and the problem this raises in Chapter 7.

(2) *Must there be a Designer?*
Does all this mean that there must be a Designer?

Unfortunately not.

It means that there *may* be a Designer. Perhaps it means that there probably is a Designer. But we cannot use the phrase 'there must be'.

There is another option open to us. We may look at the universe and maintain that it is the work of blind, mindless, chance – things just happened to work out right. Those who believe this often say that it is the disharmony (the earthquakes, etc), which leads them to this view.

One man looks at the universe and says 'I believe in God'. Despite the areas of disharmony, he maintains that only God can account for breathtaking beauty, and for the incredible number of things which work together to make life possible. Another man looks at the universe and says 'I believe in chance'. It is open to him to make this act of faith.

A study of design in the universe cannot prove beyond all doubt that God exists. The argument from design is not watertight.

If we are to get beyond the point of stalemate we must look elsewhere. In particular we must consider personal experience, and history.

God at work today

In the chapter on the resurrection we noted that a good many people maintain that God has profoundly influenced their lives – giving them moral power and peace of mind, and in some cases completely changing the course of their lives.

Those who make this sort of claim come from a wide variety of backgrounds and are of such differing temperaments, that it is very hard to argue with the explanation which they give.

If they are right – if God really has influenced their lives – then of course God exists.

We may well add to this, the fact that many people claim to have been healed physically by God. This is too big a question to go into here, but it is worth noting in passing.

We need to examine such claims very carefully. It may well be possible to explain many of these healings in other ways, but if only a handful of these people are correct in their explanation, this too points to the fact that God exists.

Jesus Christ

This is by far the most convincing argument. All we need to do here is briefly to recap two previous sections.

(1) Jesus claimed to be God. If He was, then obviously, the existence of God is proved beyond all doubt.

The New Testament expressed the Incarnation (God become man) in various ways. Sometimes it refers to the unique relationship which exists between Jesus and His 'Heavenly Father' by using the phrase 'Son of God'. The same phrase is also used to refer to those men and women who, through faith in Christ, have entered the family of God. There is, of course, a clear difference in these two uses of the phrase – it is *His* sonship which makes ours possible.

The point to note here is that the force of the argument remains, however we express it. If Jesus *is* the Son of God, then the God of whom He is the Son, must exist.

Hence the question 'Does God Exist' resolves itself into a question about Christ. As we saw in Chapter 8, if we reject His own teaching about Himself, the difficulty of finding an alternative explanation which accounts for this teaching in a satisfactory way is tremendous.

Either we accept His own estimate of Himself – and hence accept that God exists – or we must believe that He was a liar or a madman.

(2) The New Testament also claims that God raised Jesus from the dead. If this is true, we are yet again forced to the conclusion that God must exist. And so again, what appears to be a vast and difficult question about the existence of God, is in reality a historical problem about making sense of Christ and the way Christianity began.

If the evidence outlined in Chapter 9 is correct, we have our answer. God does exist. We know this because He has given us a vivid 'visual aid'.

He sent His Son to us, in the person of Jesus Christ. When men executed His Son, God raised Him from the dead.

In addition to proving God's existence, Christ shows us what God is like. 'Like Father like Son'. The keynote of His character is strong love.

In the light of this, the fact that we find design in the universe takes on a new significance. We may not believe in God *because* of design. But if we believe in God because of Christ, then we learn that the harmony and pattern is due to God after all.

Feel the firm earth under your feet and ponder the fact that it is moving in orbit through space at around 66,000 miles per hour. Look at the heavens, and remember that the light from the nearest star takes over 4 years to reach earth – and light travels at 186,282 miles per second. Consider the beautiful simplicity of the recurring pattern of the seasons. Contemplate the fact that underlying it all is a complexity so great that the world's scientists constantly need to review and revise their findings.

The God who cares for us; the God who came to us; the God with whom we can communicate in prayer; the God who will flood our individual lives with meaning and power if we will allow Him – He it is who designed, and who created, and who upholds all things.

If we can be moved by anything, this will move us. With the Psalmist we will declare

'Great is the Lord and worthy of all praise;
His greatness is unfathomable.
One generation shall commend thy works to another
and set forth thy mighty deeds' (Psalm 145. 3–4).

Books of interest

Modern Miracles by J. Winslow (Hodder and Stoughton)

God's Smuggler by Brother Andrew (Hodder and Stoughton)

Double Miracle by A. T. Skipp (Hodder and Stoughton)

CHAPTER ELEVEN

The Case against inertia

It is my conviction that the 'Case against Christ' is not a strong one. The evidence *for* Him is very strong indeed.

It is vitally important to keep the discussion about Christianity centred on this question of evidence. For either Christianity is true, or it is false.

'His hobby is gardening. My hobby is fishing. Your hobby is religion.' Such an attitude is woefully inadequate. Christianity just won't fit into a list of hobbies or interests. It is far too big.

People follow Christ for a variety of reasons. Some, because they have a keen sense of sin and know that they need forgiveness and moral power. Some because they feel inadequate to deal with life, and know that they need help.

Others because they are deeply impressed with the life of a particular Christian or group of Christians. Yet others because they read the New Testament and are convinced that Jesus Christ is the Son of God.

All these are valid reasons. But the primary reason for becoming a Christian, which underlies them all, is that *Christianity is true*.

Perhaps a personal note will be appropriate here. The *basic* reason why I am a Christian is not because I have a religious temperament (I'm not sure that I have); nor because I find it convenient (its moral teaching is often extremely *in*convenient); nor because it brings comfort (although it does); nor even because I find in it the strength which I need to live my daily life (although I do).

I am a Christian because I am convinced that Christianity is *true*. If anyone could show me that it is not true, then I would have nothing more to do with it.

We are not dealing with a matter of personal taste, but with a question of truth or falsehood. Either Jesus *is* the Son of God or He is not. Either He *did* rise from the dead or He did not.

Practical

The fact that it is a question of truth and straight thinking does not mean that Christianity is mere theory – and so without practical implications.

I discovered recently that it is quite probable that a woman in a crinoline introduced overarm bowling into cricket. It is perfectly appropriate to follow such a discovery with the phrase 'how interesting'. Other discoveries – that your house is on fire, or that you have inherited a fortune – must be followed by positive action.

The discovery that Christianity is true comes into the second category. To follow Christ because He is the Truth, involves a revolution in our behaviour and moral standards, and in our entire outlook on life.

Christ comes with tough demands.

But He comes too with unutterable comfort. In a world beset by problems He comes as guide. In a world where many are lonely, He comes as friend. To a world characterized by lack of meaning, He brings understanding. Over a world where dying is the single certainty, He sits enthroned as the Conqueror of death.

The words of Jesus have been tested and proved in the lives of countless thousands of men and women, in a way in which no other words have ever been. 'I am the way; I am the truth and I am life' (John 14. 6).